ORGANIZING WHILE UNDOCUMENTED

LATINA/O SOCIOLOGY SERIES

General Editors: Pierrette Hondagneu-Sotelo and Victor M. Rios

Family Secrets: Stories of Incest and Sexual Violence in Mexico
Gloria González-López

Deported: Immigrant Policing, Disposable Labor, and Global Capitalism
Tanya Maria Golash-Boza

From Deportation to Prison: The Politics of Immigration Enforcement in Post–Civil Rights America
Patrisia Macías-Rojas

Latina Teachers: Creating Careers and Guarding Culture
Glenda M. Flores

Citizens but Not Americans: Race and Belonging among Latino Millennials
Nilda Flores-Gonzalez

Immigrants under Threat: Risk and Resistance in Deportation Nation
Greg Prieto

Kids at Work: Latinx Families Selling Food on the Streets of Los Angeles
Emir Estrada

Organizing While Undocumented: Immigrant Youth's Political Activism under the Law
Kevin Escudero

Organizing While Undocumented

Immigrant Youth's Political Activism under the Law

Kevin Escudero

NEW YORK UNIVERSITY PRESS
New York

NEW YORK UNIVERSITY PRESS
New York
www.nyupress.org
© 2020 by New York University

Library of Congress Cataloging-in-Publication Data
Names: Escudero, Kevin, author.
Title: Organizing while undocumented : immigrant youth's political activism under the law / Kevin Escudero.
Description: New York : New York University Press, [2020] | Series: Latina/o sociology series | Includes bibliographical references and index.
Identifiers: LCCN 2019009084 | ISBN 9781479803194 (cloth) | ISBN 9781479834150 (paperback)
Subjects: LCSH: Immigrant youth—Political activity—United States. | Illegal aliens—Political activity—United States. | Immigrant youth—Civil rights—United States. | Immigrant youth—Legal status, laws, etc.—United States. | Youth protest movements—United States. | Social justice—United States.
Classification: LCC JV6477 .E73 2020 | DDC 322.086/910973—dc23
LC record available at https://lccn.loc.gov/2019009084

CONTENTS

Introduction

David, an undocumented and queer—or undocuqueer—activist living in the San Francisco Bay Area, immigrated to the United States with his parents from Mexico in the 1990s. Raised in a predominantly working-class community in Southern California, he excelled in school and ranked at the top of his high school graduating class. Eager to continue his upward educational trajectory, David applied and was accepted to the state's top public university. To help defer the high cost of attending college as an undocumented student, David first attended his local community college and then reapplied for admission to the public university to which he had been accepted a few years earlier. After being accepted to the university once more and graduating from college, David completed a prestigious fellowship examining the intersections of queer and undocumented immigrant identities and later matriculated into a PhD program in the humanities. While on the surface it may seem that David's social mobility and educational success occurred in a largely linear fashion and that both his undocumented and queer identities played an equal role in his understanding of his own identity, this was not the case. Rather, David's immigration status and sexual orientation held differing roles during the various phases of his life. In fact, as David described, it was through his activism and experience in college that he came to embrace his identities and put them into action as part of his social movement participation.

During David's childhood, his immigration status was not something he discussed with his family or with others in his community: "Growing up in Southern California as an undocumented immigrant, my immigration status was not something my family or others in our community placed much attention [on]." David, his parents, and his extended family all shared a common undocumented status and thus a mutual understanding of how the status shaped the specific opportunities that were available to them. And, while David's immigration status was not the primary factor in his life growing up, something else was: his sexual orientation.

David later relayed how, unlike his immigration status, his sexual orientation created tension in his household during his childhood given his parents' initial opposition to his sexuality. This disagreement was significant in defining how David understood his own identity and his relationships to others around him. It was not until David applied to college, which he chose by focusing on schools that had a reputation for being "queer friendly," that he learned about the full implications of his undocumented immigrant status: "It wasn't until I graduated high school and applied to colleges that I realized what being undocumented meant. Coming out as a gay man predominated much of my high school and teenage years, but in college, surrounded by an undocumented and queer community, I began to think more deeply about what it meant to be both queer and undocumented." Thus, David not only began to realize the full implications of his undocumented status as he navigated the college admissions process but also began to consider how he might be able to combine his identities both as a gay man and an undocumented immigrant. While he knew that these two identities converged for him on a daily basis in terms of how he navigated certain social and educational spaces, it was only when he matriculated at college that he developed a framework for combining the two:

> [In college] I started seeing how in my own organizing and involvement with different organizations on campus that I was really dividing my identity up into these spaces. My work at the Gender Equity Resource Center meant being gay; my work as part of the Chicano Latino Student Development office meant being a person of color; and organizing in the Multicultural Immigrant Student Program meant being an immigrant. [Eventually] . . . I . . . started engaging with a lot of feminist of color thought [and] this mindset began to change. It really got me thinking and just processing what it meant to be undocumented, what it means for me to be a student of color or what it means for me to be queer. It's something that I feel very fragmented about because I can't find that common ground for myself that while I try to be inclusive with my identity it's something that I still don't know how to do.[1]

By drawing from the academic frameworks he was exposed to as part of his gender and sexuality studies coursework, David learned

[Handwritten margin note: Same dialogue, looking for POC friendly Schools]

about the experiences of other community members—immigrant women, queer communities of color, and others—who faced similar challenges in confronting the marginalization they faced as a result of holding multiple social identities. A student activist on campus, he diligently worked to bring together discussions of queer experiences and immigrant narratives as part of the work he engaged in on campus. Following his graduation from college, David spent a year on a research fellowship working with other self-identified undocuqueer organizers to build community and engage one another, using the arts and visual culture as a mechanism for doing so. He has continued to engage in this work upon enrolling in graduate school, with a greater focus on the arts as a mechanism for social movement participation and community building.

At first glance, David's experience may seem unique and potentially an isolated case of a high-achieving undocumented and queer activist. *utilizing an intersectional framework* Yet, as I argue in this book, in their activism, undocumented immigrant youth have, as a whole, emphasized the importance of an intersectional identity. From my interviews with and observations of members of the undocumented immigrant community, I learned that for these activists, an intersectional identity—an identity informed by the various ways they self-identified and which were tied to systems of injustice and inequality—offered a critical framework from which to understand how these community members approached and conducted their activism.[2] In light of the number of undocumented immigrant activists who, like David, identified as members of more than one marginalized community, this book asks: *How do undocumented immigrant youth,* *Guided question* *a community that is criminalized under the law, utilize their multiple identities—racial, gender, legal status, and sexual orientation—and these identities' intersections in the formation of a social movement?* As the evidence presented in this book demonstrates, undocumented immigrant activists strategically employ an intersectional movement identity to counteract the legal limitations they face in organizing due to their undocumented immigrant status. In doing so, these activists simultaneously work to build coalitions with members of other similarly situated communities.

A Portrait of Undocumented Immigrant Youth

While mainstream media have depicted undocumented immigrant youth as largely a monolithic entity, this community comprises a diverse set of people and experiences. Within immigration scholarship, the term "undocumented" has been understood as referring to those individuals who do not hold formal recognition under the law. Of the approximately 11.2 million undocumented immigrants residing in the United States, 2.1 million are estimated to be youth under the age of eighteen.[3] These youth are members of what has been termed the "1.5 generation," or individuals who arrived in the United States at a young age and spent their adolescence in the country.[4] Undocumented status has been vitally important to the assimilation and acculturation processes these youth undergo, as well as to their ability to make particular rights claims.[5]

Members of the undocumented community primarily enter the United States through one of two ways: (1) with a passport and a valid visa (such as a tourist, student, or temporary work visa) or (2) without a visa and not through an official port of entry. Contrary to depictions of undocumented immigrants crossing the border on a whim and never having applied for any formal documentation status, recent estimates find that the majority of undocumented immigrants are "visa over-stayers," entering legally and then becoming undocumented at a later point.[6] Lapsing into undocumented status may also occur when families seek to adjust their status but are unable to do so and, as a result, are issued an order of deportation. Given the lengthy wait times and the high cost of the US immigration process, many undocumented people are issued orders of deportation after living in the country for an ex-tended period and having established family networks and social ties. While members of these two groups—those who entered with a visa and those who did not—ultimately have different legal options for adjusting their status, they are subjected to similar forms of social and political disenfranchisement.

In terms of racial/ethnic identity, research has shown that the major-ity of undocumented immigrants in the United States, approximately 75 percent, come from Latin America (with Mexico being the coun-try that has sent the most undocumented immigrants to the United States).[7] Though a smaller population, Asian undocumented migration has occurred, alongside Latinx undocumented migration, for quite some time.[8] Making up an estimated 13 percent of the approximately 11.2 million undocumented immigrants nationally, undocumented Asian immigrants have been well represented in higher education but have gained less visibility overall as compared with their Latinx counterparts.[9] Notably, historians have chronicled how Asian migrants were some of the first undocumented people, coming to the United States during the Chinese exclusion era (1882–1943) using false documents and claiming nonexistent family ties to strangers or entering through Latin America.[10] Recently, in the University of California system, one of the nation's largest public higher education systems, almost half of the undocumented students filing affidavits to pay in-state tuition come from Asia.[11] The navigation of racial/ethnic boundaries and identities *interlocking* is an important axis along which undocumented people have worked *axis of* to highlight the unique experiences of particular intersectional iden- *oppression* tity formations within the larger undocumented community and how undocumented status can serve as an effective identity category under which communities can mobilize.

This demographic overview provides important context for understanding the experiences of undocumented adults and youth, but their narratives can be further contextualized through an analysis of the subjective experience of being undocumented in the United States today. Scholars in history and the social sciences, particularly sociology and anthropology, have offered the concept of migrant illegality to explain the deleterious effects of undocumented status on undocumented migrants' everyday lives.[12] Migrant illegality is thus a concept that is vast in its ability to explain the impact of immigration status in constraining opportunities—social, educational, and otherwise.[13] Elaborating on the term and its meaning, anthropologist Nicholas DeGenova writes: "Indeed, 'illegalizations'—or . . . the legal production of migrant 'illegality'—supply the foundational conditions of possibility . . . that institute an official adjustment of status for the undocumented. Every 'illegalization' implies the possibility of its own rectification. Once we recognize that undocumented migrations are constituted in order not to physically exclude [undocumented migrants] but instead, to socially include them under imposed conditions of enforced and protracted vulnerability, it is not difficult to fathom how migrants' endurance of many years of 'illegality' can serve as disciplinary apprenticeship in the subordination of their labor."[14] As DeGenova's articulation of the term makes clear, illegality's effects are far-reaching, with implications in the most intimate spheres of migrants' everyday lives. As I argue in this book, while one might suspect that this form of physical and social exclusion would make life impossible, what some have referred to as social death, undocumented immigrants have organized powerful countermobilizations to resist the stigma of illegality.[15] These countermobilizations have included significant representation from undocumented immigrant youth who occupy a unique social and legal positioning facilitating their ability to be hyperaware of the injustices they and their fellow community members face and also to be well situated to voice opposition to such oppression.

Undocumented Youth at the Forefront of the Immigrant Rights Movement

Due to their exclusion from accessing formal legal status in the United States, undocumented immigrants are considered by some to be a group of "unlikely political actors." As the scholarly literature on migrant illegality has aptly pointed out, immigrant legal status manifests in multiple ways and has a myriad of implications for the lives of undocumented immigrants.[16] Yet, despite these barriers, undocumented individuals have been active in movements to counteract the stigmatizing and criminalizing effects of migrant illegality.[17] In this work scholars have examined the importance of frameworks related to the family unit, labor, religion, and education in understanding how illegality manifests and in minimizing its deleterious effects.[18]

Undocumented immigrant youth are a key subgroup within the undocumented immigrant community. As members of the 1.5 generation, undocumented immigrant youth occupy a unique social and legal positioning, which I argue has led to their success as social movement activists and leaders.[19] In particular, two aspects of these young people's social and legal positioning are important in explaining their high level of participation in social movement activism: (1) their political socialization within the US education system and (2) their coming of age as beneficiaries of the US Supreme Court's decision in *Plyler v. Doe*.[20]

As members of the 1.5 generation, undocumented youth were born abroad and immigrated to the United States, often with their families, prior to adolescence. As a result, these young people have been socialized within the US education system, a system that instills familiarity with the American political system and provides a broad narrative of its use as a tool for underrepresented communities seeking access to increased rights.[21] Such framings of the legal system as a mechanism meant to bring about social change have, in turn, shaped undocumented immigrant youth's interest in politics and their view of the system as one that can provide a path to greater political representation.

Today's generation of undocumented immigrant youth are also beneficiaries of *Plyler v. Doe*.[22] As *Plyler* beneficiaries, undocumented youth have been provided access to a free, public K-12 education, an educational experience that is similar to that of their US citizen peers. Yet, upon graduation from high school, their protection as minors and individuals with access to rights largely similar to those of their US citizen peers is disrupted.[23] Facing these newfound barriers and being familiar with a system that has worked for them in the past, many undocumented young people not only see promise in the US political system but also see participation and use of its mechanisms as rights that should be made available to them as well.

Moreover, two critical political moments have facilitated undocumented youth's assumption of a leadership role alongside other members of the undocumented immigrant community: activism around the Development, Relief, and Education for Alien Minors (DREAM) Act, which was first introduced in 2001, and the immigrant rights marches of May 2006.[24] Having worked with social movement activists in Southern California, Walter Nicholls detailed in his book *The DREAMers* the emergence of a unifying undocumented immigrant youth identity, which he argued was part of active movement-building efforts involving a variety of individuals and organizations and taking advantage of niche openings in the political and legal landscape. He explained: "Undocumented youths around the country, with the assistance of immigrant rights associations, formed college campus support groups, advocacy organizations in their communities, online networks through blogs, Facebook, Twitter and so on, and national organizations. . . . Individual youth began to learn that they were not alone. They learned that there were hundreds and thousands of people in a very similar situation and that they were all facing common hopes, obstacles, fears and dreams."[25] Similarly, working with undocumented youth in Orange County, California, sociologist Roberto G. Gonzales explained how undocumented Latinx youth, a previously largely untapped political force, mobilized to participate in the immigrant rights marches of May 2006 largely due to their previous involvement in other social movements, which led them to "turn inward and . . . take steps towards organizing for themselves [and their communities]."[26] Thus, as Nicholls's and Gonzales's work demonstrates, the increasing political power of undocumented youth and the strategic ways that these young people marshaled their growing influence to fight for increased rights represent a turning point in the broader immigrant rights movement.

Scholars of undocumented immigrant youth activism have also focused on the strategies that youth developed to push their cause forward. One of the key ways this has occurred was undocumented youth's adoption of the "coming-out" strategy, drawing on tactics employed by LGBTQ activists.[27] "Coming out" refers to the process of disclosing one's undocumented status, similar to the disclosure LGBTQ individuals make when sharing their sexual orientation, usually in a public manner. Another important repertoire that activists highlighted is the role of storytelling, both in person and digital, in distributing their message to a broader audience.[28] Scholars writing on this topic have additionally discussed the role of legal status, when considered alongside other identities in an educational context, as well as the intersection of sexuality and immigrant status.[29]

This book departs in three primary ways from this earlier research on the political activism of undocumented immigrant youth. First, while researchers have noted the multiple axes of marginalization—race, class, and gender—that youth face and their combined impact on young people's educational experiences, this book extends the conversation into the realm of social movement activism and organizing. In doing so, it articulates the ways activists have utilized these multiple identities as assets in their social movement participation. Second, this book examines the use of intersectionality as a social movement strategy across multiple contexts—Asian undocumented, undocuqueer, and formerly undocumented activists' participation in the contemporary immigrant rights movement—to illustrate how intersectional identities are not relegated to a particular subset of the undocumented immigrant community but span multiple communities within the movement. Third, through the theorization of the Identity Mobilization Model, this book offers a framework to examine the political activism of groups whose identities and lived experiences have been used as a resource to contest the law's delegitimizing effects. In the context of the immigrant rights movement, this phenomenon has been characterized by what scholars have termed "migrant illegality," the violence of the law and the legal system, and the law's role as a "master status" in undocumented immigrants' daily lives.[30]

Highlighting the case of undocumented immigrant youth's multiple subjectivities, this book illustrates how this previously untapped group of social movement organizers not only recognized their power but put it into practice. In doing so, the book contributes to broader conversations taking place in sociology, anthropology, education, and law regarding the impact of and operationalization of migrant illegality, the role of identity in social movement activism, and organizers' ability to build coalitions with members of similarly situated groups. By focusing on the plight of undocumented youth, I demonstrate how these young people are, in fact, fighting for increased rights for all immigrants and the various communities with which these individuals identify. These organizers are thus developing a template for future organizing not only by undocumented immigrant youth but also by other groups that have been legally disenfranchised under the US legal system.

The Case for an Intersectional Movement Identity

Acknowledging the diverse array of experiences encompassed by the term "undocumented immigrant," *Organizing While Undocumented* explains how undocumented youth, assumed by some to be an unlikely set of political actors, were and continue to be key constituents in the immigrant rights movement. This story highlights youth's agency in the development of organizing strategies and tactics, placing attention on the community's awareness of the law and legal system's benefits and limitations as they work within the law to dismantle its marginalizing effects. In this process, I argue that undocumented youth have crafted an intersectional social movement identity as an alternative to the law's criminalizing framework that emphasizes legal status as an individual's primary social identity.

Subjected to the federal government's criminalization of their status and the threat of removal for participating in social movement activism, they have experiences, one could argue, that are comparable to those of other similarly situated communities in the United States and on the global stage. Yet, as members of the 1.5 generation, these youth have spent the majority of their lives in the United States and see themselves as entitled to all the rights and privileges accorded to US citizens. This book focuses on the experiences of undocumented immigrant youth who inhabit a unique social and legal position—and one of considerable political power.

In her frequently cited article "Up the Anthropologist: Perspectives Gained from Studying Up," Laura Nader argues that anthropologists have much to contribute to understandings of power and those who hold it. While this approach is often employed to study societal elites, in *Organizing While Undocumented* I focus on the experiences of undocumented immigrant youth who are members of a marginalized group that has come to wield significant political power. Employing a grassroots perspective, recentering activist voices and experiences as a means of "studying up," blurs the boundaries between the traditional idea of who holds power and the potential impact of grassroots social movement activists. Such an approach is central to an exploration of marginalized communities' participation in social movement activism, reframing community experiences that speak to dominant legal discourse.[31]

Ultimately, I argue that undocumented immigrant youth represent a uniquely positioned group of activists who face grave consequences for their participation in social movement activism: removal from the state via detention and deportation. Rather than acquiesce to the law's criminalizing effects, undocumented immigrant youth have strategically and intentionally deployed an intersectional counternarrative to reframe how they are depicted and made legible under the law. Using the framework of the Identity Mobilization Model, this book details the specific processes through which undocumented immigrant youth deploy an intersectional lens to understand immigrant activist identity, providing an overarching understanding of the macro- and micro-level processes through which social change occurs. As a result, this book illuminates how activists have successfully exploited openings in the political opportunity structure to build coalitions with members of other similarly situated groups and communities.   *coalition building*

Methodology

In conducting research for this book, I drew on ethnographic participant observation and fifty-one in-depth interviews conducted with undocumented immigrant activists in San Francisco, Chicago, and New York City. As discussed in the following chapter, these three cities were chosen based on their similarity in terms of proportion of residents who are undocumented and their shared status as global immigrant gateway cities. Fieldwork in San Francisco and Chicago was conducted from 2010 to 2014, with additional and follow-up interviews taking place from 2014 to 2019.[32] I spent extended periods in the book's third site, New York City, from 2015 to 2018, attending key public-facing events hosted by immigrant rights organizations that explored various aspects of undocumented immigrant experiences and conducting interviews with activists I met through my participation in the broader movement. To recruit participants in each city, I used a snowball sampling approach, making contacts with an initial set of activists and later asking them to refer me to others they knew who might also be interested in participating in the project. This method helped ensure that the individuals I interviewed were active in the communities and networks about which I hoped to learn. I began the snowball approach at multiple nodes within each geographic location to vary the networks to which interviewees belong.

Given the prevalence of multiple organizations in each city focusing on issues related to immigrant rights organizing, I chose to work with a variety of organizations, prioritizing those that were grassroots and led by undocumented immigrant youth. Doing so drew upon my interest in focusing on the activism of groups that centered undocumented immigrant narratives as a means of modeling self-determination rooted in community needs. Thus, the organizations from which I recruited interviewees were (1) led by undocumented immigrants; (2) regionally based (greater San Francisco Bay Area, Chicago area, or New York City area); and (3) identity-based (Asian undocumented students, undocuqueer communities, and undocumented youth in a particular region). This approach facilitated greater heterogeneity in terms of participant age range, the type of college or university participants attended (community college, private four-year university, and public four-year university), and the neighborhood of the city in which they resided. For further information on participants' demographic backgrounds, see appendix A.

The research collection phase of this project also took place during a period of shifting legal contexts and climates wherein some subfederal entities were passing legislation to uphold the rights of undocumented immigrants, and others were passing legislation to curtail rights allocated to this community.[33] Yet, as explain in chapter 1, all three cities in which fieldwork for this book was conducted were largely welcoming, pro-immigrant urban centers. While research for this book was conducted primarily during the period leading up to the Trump administration's formal ending of the DACA program, the last phase overlapped with the undocumented immigrant community's efforts to keep the program in place.[34] At the time of the writing of this book, the DACA program remained ongoing, accepting applicants for renewal but not first-time applications; it continues to do so pending ongoing litigation.[35]

The Identity Mobilization Model

This book's primary organizing framework, the Identity Mobilization Model, offers an innovative approach for explaining political mobilization among communities that find themselves in a vulnerable legal and political position, such as undocumented immigrants. In particular, the model explains undocumented immigrant organizers' cultivation and use of an intersectional movement identity that recognizes their shared oppression as undocumented immigrants while also acknowledging activists' intersectional lived realities. While this book focuses on a case study of the contemporary immigrant rights movement, I argue that it can be used to examine other instances of activism by members of similarly situated groups that are organizing in oppressive legal environments. These other groups consist of individuals whose identities are invalidated under the law and who must first establish their presence and their right to exist before making rights claims.[36]

Informed both by the literature and by sustained ethnographic field-work with undocumented immigrant activists, I developed the Identity Mobilization Model. The model consists of three strategies that undocumented persons and members of other similarly situated groups utilize to make their rights claims legible: (1) sharing histories of community struggles with other communities to form a larger collective; (2) strategically leveraging identities of community members, highlighting moments of shared, overlapping, and intersecting experiences; and (3) calling into action allies who are viewed by the state as "legitimate political actors." For an extended discussion of the model, a diagram of its steps, and a discussion of conditions under which it applies see chapter 1, "The Identity Mobilization Model: The Strategic Utility of an Intersectional Movement Identity." Activists can draw on strategies simultaneously and at different moments in their political campaigns. Additionally, all three groups discussed in this book—Asian undocumented, queer undocumented, and formerly undocumented individuals—engage all three strategies of the Identity Mobilization Model.

Contributing to interdisciplinary social movement literature that discusses the importance of collective identity formation for movement success, the Identity Mobilization Model explores not only how collective identity is formed but also how it is maintained and leveraged. Collective identity has been an important area of research, especially for those studying what have been referred to as "new social movements." Describing collective identity as a set of common bonds across a group of people points to the similarity and difference that may exist among those who see themselves, for political purposes, as being part of a unified, collective identity. Sociologists Francesca Polletta and James Jasper write, "We have defined collective identity as an individual's cognitive, moral and emotional connection with a broader community, category, practice or institution."[37] Thus, while collective identity includes multiple sets of ties that individuals enjoy and share, there can also exist variation in how this identity is lived and experienced, or in how it operates in conjunction with other identities that activists hold.

Given that, as Polletta and Jasper have noted, collective identity can be conceived of as filling in gaps left by structural theories such as the resource mobilization and political process models, while structural mechanisms remain an important area of study, in this book I pay attention to the micro-level processes and their interaction with macro-level structures such as legal frames and norms.[38] Addressing the challenge of studying collective identity and its impact on structural forces that affect community political mobilization, the Identity Mobilization Model examines collective identity intersectionally. In doing so, it takes up Polletta and Jasper's challenge of relating the individual and the structural as two key terrains that activists negotiate in their mobilization of a social movement. Also, rather than solely emphasizing the necessity for movement activists to work toward the construction of an overarching identity, I illustrate how the multiple subgroups within a given movement can be an asset to achieving the movement's goals.

These identity-based and legally grounded strategies are combined in the model to illustrate how undocumented immigrant activists counter the law's criminalizing effects on their community while simultaneously framing this struggle as part of a broader interconnected rights struggle. As such, this challenge of exerting rights under a hostile legal regime is one that groups positioned similarly to undocumented immigrants also face. Although this study focuses primarily on undocumented communities and related groups—Asian American immigrant communities, and the LGBTQ community—this model, I argue, can also potentially be applied to other groups that experience similar legally based forms of discrimination. The model is transformative, bringing into consideration a type of politics that was previously considered, as Amalia Pallares describes, "impossible," in that it allows activist groups to move away from an interest-group movement and reframe their organizing as concerned with larger frames of justice and inclusion in the nation-state or, in some instances, beyond the nation-state.[39]

Overview of the Book

This book begins by introducing readers to its central theoretical contribution: the Identity Mobilization Model, which offers a three-part framework for understanding how undocumented immigrant activists use an intersectional movement identity to overcome legal and structural barriers to organizing. The model delineates three specific strategies activists have drawn upon in their organizing—(1) community knowledge–sharing practices, (2) strategic leveraging of an intersectional identity, and (3) high-stakes allyship—to demonstrate how undocumented immigrants are able to make their rights claims legible within the mainstream political sphere. In the first chapter I also explain how the model and its steps serve as a blueprint for the book's remaining chapters. The later chapters focus on how all three groups—Asian undocumented, undocuqueer. and formerly undocumented individuals—engage these three steps of the model.

Chapter 1 also includes an overview of the subfederal legal landscape in the three cities in which I conducted research for the book: San Francisco, Chicago, and New York. This discussion is accompanied by an overview of the history of each of the three movement subgroups whose participation in the immigrant rights movement is the focus of the book. Combined, the information serves as a road map that offers key contextual information for readers as they approach the ethnographic and interview-based chapters that follow. While these later data-driven chapters explain how these processes evolved in social movement activism, chapter 1 provides a central organizing model, informed by robust theoretical frameworks, to assist readers in understanding the full scope and impact of the organizing in which these youth have engaged.

Chapter 2 focuses on the case of Asian undocumented youth to explain community efforts to unearth the silenced history of Asian undocumented migration and to place this history in relation to current immigration debates. As part of these efforts, activists use storytelling strategies to counteract stereotypes of Asian immigrants as solely high-skilled workers and individuals who have come to the United States to attend college, noting that Asians were and continue to be affected by the issue of undocumented immigration. Asian undocumented activists also strategically draw upon their intersectional identities in Latinx organizing spaces to work alongside members of a group that is largely invoked in the national imaginary in discussions regarding undocumented immigration. Extending activists' efforts to build on discussions of the increased representation of Asian and other non-Latinx undocumented activists in the movement, this chapter discusses the extensive efforts that Asian and Latinx undocumented organizers have undertaken to emphasize the importance of employing a broad, multiracial approach to framing undocumented immigrant identity. I conclude this chapter with an examination of my own experience as an ally with Asian undocumented people in a high-stakes context, illustrating how sharing knowledge can lead to high-stakes allyship.

Chapter 3 focuses on the experiences of undocuqueer activists, or those who identify as both undocumented and queer.[40] Undocuqueer activist narratives, like the narratives of Asian undocumented movement participants, illustrate the importance of a heterogeneous movement identity while emphasizing the utility of such an approach in building coalitions with members of similarly situated communities. Undocuqueer individuals in San Francisco, Chicago, and New York City who participated in this research project began their explanation of their work by drawing parallels between the "coming-out" processes that members in both communities have undergone. Activists also highlighted the differences in the function and stakes of the coming-out experience for these two communities and the unique, layered effects this poses for undocuqueer-identified individuals. Emphasizing the manner in which undocuqueer organizers have taken a critical role at the forefront of the national immigrant rights movement, this chapter discusses how undocuqueer activists have leveraged their intersectional identities to increase the visibility of queer issues in immigrant rights organizing spaces and vice versa. Finally, allyship by queer individuals who experience marginalization but are also US citizens is a topic that undocuqueer activists draw upon as they work to increase the visibility and to promote the specific needs of their community within the larger immigrant rights movement.

Profiling a group of individuals whose experiences are not often covered within the literature on undocumented migration, chapter 4 highlights the narratives of formerly undocumented individuals who have continued their involvement in the immigrant rights movement after adjusting their immigration status. By including the case of formerly undocumented individuals in discussions of undocumented immigrant activism, this chapter draws attention to the fluid, shifting nature of legal status and the continuum rather than the divide between "directly affected movement participants" and allies. In the Supreme Court's 1982 opinion in *Plyler v. Doe*, the justices envisioned undocumented status as temporary, limited to a given point in an individual's life. Through introducing the experiences of formerly undocumented individuals into the scholarly discussions of undocumented immigration, this chapter high-lights the lingering effects of being undocumented for individuals who are able to adjust their immigration status and its role in shaping their continued participation in the movement. Within the subgroup of for-merly undocumented activists, chapter 4 focuses on the case of formerly undocumented women of color organizers. These activists' experiences highlight the gendered and racialized nature of migration and ties to the construction of a formerly undocumented activist contingent within the immigrant rights movement. This chapter also points out that allyship, when enacted by formerly undocumented individuals, is not necessarily as clear-cut as it might initially seem. As such, the chapter underscores the need for a reconceptualization of the role of allies in identity-based activist movements and the potential for this untapped resource within a given movement. In each of these ethnographic chapters, I demonstrate how each subgroup makes use of the same three strategies identified in the Identity Mobilization Model in slightly different ways. Their com-mon usage of these strategies speaks to the durability of the strategies and their centrality to this organizing.

Organizing While Undocumented concludes with an analysis of how the Identity Mobilization Model can speak to ongoing debates within the social movement literature about the importance and necessity of coalition building and the strategies by which it is achieved. The con-clusion also addresses contemporary developments in the ongoing fight for immigrant rights as a means of understanding the movement's fu-ture and its promise to bring about meaningful, transformative social change for migrants and marginalized communities more broadly. Consequently, this book can be read as illuminating challenges in the contemporary political moment, when state-sanctioned policies target multiple communities, including undocumented immigrants, Muslim individuals, and working-class people of color. Movements for social justice will continue to be relevant as communities move toward the dismantling of oppressive power structures. To do so, they will need to consider the utility of a coalitionary structure to advance a cause, working within and going beyond the nation-state framework in the process. Establishing a basis from which to assert rights in this environ-ment is key, but equally important are collaboration and coordination with others facing similar challenges. Asking us to consider the potential and limits of coalition-building work in a social movement context, *Organizing While Undocumented* centers the intersectional identities and experiences of community members doing the much-needed work to bridge discussions among those with power and those seeking to redistribute it.

1

The Identity Mobilization Model

Strategic Uses of an Intersectional Movement Identity

Acknowledging the central importance of undocumented immigrant activists' intersectional lived experiences, this book foregrounds a discussion of undocumented youth's multiple social and legal identities as a primary basis on which social movement strategies employed in their political activism are developed.[1] In fact, like David, whose narrative opened the introduction, many of the activists I interacted with across this book's three sites—San Francisco, Chicago, and New York City—emphasized the importance of an intersectional identity as part of their organizing. Drawing on the lived experiences of undocumented immigrant activists and scholarship of intersectional theorists, this book argues that the cultivation of an intersectional movement identity is a tool that organizers have used to (1) affirm heterogeneity among movement participants and (2) assist in the formation of coalitions with members of other similarly situated groups.[2] The following chapters also demonstrate how through the deployment of these movement strategies, activists have connected their personal lived experiences with a critique of the broader structures that have produced such marginalization.

Intersectionality in the contemporary immigrant rights movement has played an important role in furthering the activism of undocumented immigrant youth, both as a lens for examining the marginalization that organizers have faced and as a framework for understanding how shared oppression can lead to coalition and solidarity building.[3] An understanding of the intersectional nature of a movement participant's personal identity helps lay the foundation for an examination of how oppression on a personal level often has its roots in interconnected, overlapping systems of structural inequality. Through working to forge coalitions with members of similarly situated groups, movement participants can often begin their political activism with a desire to improve their personal and community plight, and, in the process, come to see with greater clarity the interconnected nature of the marginalization they and others face, resulting in a structural critique of the status quo.

Scholars have explored intersectional identity frameworks primarily in terms of the emergence of post-1960s identity-based social movements, often referred to as "new social movements."[4] Movements in this period that employed an intersectional approach included LGBTQ, civil rights, women's liberation, and community of color mobilizations.[5] Social science research on these movements and their use of an intersectional framework has focused primarily on activists' emphasis on complicating "single-issue" depictions of their movements. Yet, as the Identity Mobilization Model demonstrates, it is important and necessary to examine participants' strategic and intentional use of such an approach to complicate the agenda of their particular movement and to build coalitions with members of other similarly situated groups.[6]

First articulated by black feminist scholar-activists, the concept of intersectionality originated in the lived experiences of individuals who theorized directly from their daily lives and collective community experiences.[7] More recently, beginning in the 1980s and 1990s, thinkers such as legal scholar Kimberlé Crenshaw have worked to operationalize the term and incorporate the framework into mainstream academic discourse. As sociologists Dorothy Roberts and Sujatha Jesudason explain, intersectionality can be understood as providing a framework that "enables us to analyze how structures of privilege and disadvantage, such as gender, race, and class, interact in the lives of all people, depending on their particular identities and social positions."[8] Intersectionality thus functions as a key framework for understanding how oppression manifests in the daily lives of marginalized community members and provides a useful rubric for understanding how community members draw on their personal manifestations of inequality and connect them to broader efforts to counteract the structural nature of inequality. This structural inequality is rooted in unequal power relations between members of different groups and these groups' relationship to the state.

Roberts and Jesudason have importantly applied intersectional frameworks to social movement activism and in doing so have stressed intersectionality's role in facilitating coalition-building efforts between members of marginalized communities. Describing this aspect of intersectional activism, they explain that this coalition building is accomplished by "acknowledging the lived experiences and power differentials that keep [groups] apart" and "enabl[ing] discussions among groups that illuminate their similarities and values."[9] The connection of intersectional frameworks to solidarity and coalition building is indicative of the type of social movement mobilization that this book captures and uses as evidence for the creation of the Identity Mobilization Model.[10] Similarly, in her work on the black queer community, political scientist Cathy Cohen underscores the importance of interrogating the meanings of identity categories as part of broader efforts to bring about a radical and transformative movement agenda.[11] Cohen finds that both a critical analysis of a group's identity and the heterogeneity within that identity category serve as critical starting points for conversations on how to redistribute power. Through this process, Cohen advocates remaking of identity categories as a means of redistributing and reorienting power. As she writes: "We need not base our politics in the dissolution of all categories and communities, but we need instead to work toward the destabilization and remaking of our identities. Difference, in and of itself—even that difference designated through named categories—is not the problem. . . . The reconceptualization not only of the content of identity categories, but the intersectional nature of identities themselves, must become part of our political practice."[12] Collectively, these scholars' insights point to the critical importance of an intersectional identity on the individual level, the potential for an intersectional identity to facilitate coalition building, and the opportunity for coalition building and movement organizing to work to destabilize and reconfigure these very identity categories that brought community members together in the first place.

Building on these foundational theoretical approaches, the Identity Mobilization Model functions as a road map to the organization of the following three ethnographic chapters, each of which explains how a subgroup in the immigrant rights movement utilizes an intersectional movement identity to cultivate an intersectional collective identity to overcome legal and political barriers to activism. In the process, undocumented immigrant activists not only have named and affirmed the importance of utilizing an intersectional frame when advancing their movement but also have used the oppositional consciousness that such an approach facilitates to build coalitions with members of other similarly situated groups. Through this process activists named, critiqued, and worked to counteract the oppressive power structures that lead to their marginalized identities.

The Identity Mobilization Model Framework

The Identity Mobilization Model illustrates the coming together of a diverse set of individuals and the simultaneous forging of a collective identity that affirms difference while at the same time facilitating the formation of a united front.[13] In engaging in this research, I noticed that the individuals I worked with were a group of activists who saw identity as an important reason for their participation in political organizing and identify as activists. Through these shared positionings and entry into the movement vis-à-vis social movement organizations, these activists, who enacted the strategies outlined in this model, ultimately ended up working across movement organizations and identity subgroups to create a multifaceted, intersectional collective identity.

As undocumented youth have operationalized the use of their intersectional identities, they have also worked to refashion how a collective identity can function for a social movement. Collective identity is a theoretical framework that emerged from the need to more closely examine the factors affecting how individuals mobilize and the circumstances that have facilitated such action.[14] For members of marginalized groups, collective identity is a critical tool for establishing a successful social movement and ensuring its longevity. At the same time, multiple levels of marginalization often exist among members of a marginalized group.[15] Drawing on the activism of undocumented immigrant youth, the Identity Mobilization Model illustrates how a broader approach to examining the form collective identities take and their uses by social movement participants can open new avenues for understanding the structure and dynamics of political mobilization.[16]

Some social movement scholars have argued that movements with weak or diffuse collective identities are unable to achieve buy-in from potential participants and are therefore less successful in changing the status quo.[17] This book argues that an affirmation of movement participants' multiple social identities can in fact be an asset.[18] More-over, while scholars have importantly made the case that the forma-tion of a movement's collective identity is central to the process of ensuring cohesion and building momentum to advance the move-ment's cause, further discussion is needed regarding the role of inter-sectional movement identities as part of such organizing efforts.[19] The model also works to counteract the critique of identity-based move-ments that they are short-lived and that once a movement's goal is achieved, a given identity category becomes irrelevant and so does the movement.

Key to *Organizing While Undocumented*'s examination of undocu-mented immigrant youth's use of an intersectional movement identity is a tripartite conceptualization of the law. In this book I argue for a three-part conceptualization of the law in which it serves as (1) a social identity, (2) a tool for *and* target of activism, and (3) a set of cultural meanings and beliefs.[20] This lays the groundwork for an analysis of an intersectional approach to social movement activism at the individual and structural levels.[21]

Legal mobilization scholars have focused on the role of the law in social movement activism, discussing individuals' everyday theori-zations of and experiences with the law. As sociolegal studies scholar Anna-Maria Marshall explains, this field of study began with a focus on the formal, institutionalized conceptions of law and gradually shifted toward a more fluid, constructivist formulation. A constructivist ap-proach to the law can help create space for an analysis of the law at the structural and individual levels. The law for undocumented immigrant youth therefore does not function as a static entity but acts as a socially constructed identity operating on multiple registers. Sociolegal studies research has also largely been animated by questions of whether the law is a tool for activism or the target of activism.[22] Yet, as this book demon-strates, the law can function as both a tool for and a target of activism. Acknowledging the unique positioning of the undocumented commu-nity and its treatment under the law points to the federal government's use of the law to disenfranchise undocumented people, contrasted with the community's countermobilization to secure legal rights guaranteed under the law. This grassroots community mobilization and the law's criminalizing effects occur within a cultural context wherein laws are passed and function at the level of the citizen's comprehension of fairness, justice, and equality.

In the diagram in figure 1.1, groups that are positioned similarly in terms of the legal order but do not view themselves as part of the same struggle are represented by disparate shapes. Over time, these groups gradually begin to look more similar to one another. Through enacting the specific strategies outlined in the model, activists begin to emphasize their shared interests and connections. In doing so, similarities between groups or subgroups become increasingly evident, and a greater awareness of the overlapping nature of identity becomes apparent to the viewer as seen in the second strategy: the strategic leveraging of an intersectional identity. The third strategy—building power through high-stakes allyship—points to the linked fate of groups and how a strong connection exists between the successes of one marginalized group fighting oppression and a combined coalition of groups working together and pooling resources.

For individuals who are denied access to certain legal and political rights, as is relevant in the case of undocumented immigrant community members, the model's three strategies provide an understanding of how such an identity is cultivated and utilized to secure access to such rights. These strategies assist scholars in analyzing the use and cultivation of an intersectional movement identity among social movement participants to meet a particular set of end goals. As noted earlier while interrelated, these strategies are not necessarily sequential. Rather, they can be utilized in any order, but, as the following sections illustrate, are all present in the activism of the three subgroups covered in this book.

The model's first strategy—community knowledge–sharing practices—explains how groups that are often seen as having different interests within the mainstream political sphere come together and organize through learning about the shared, overlapping nature of their marginalizing experiences. This concept can contribute to a broader interest by social movement scholars regarding the formation, duration, and nature of "social ties" among movement participants and the role of such ties in facilitating coalition building among members of different movement constituencies.[23] More specifically, community knowledge–sharing practices are grassroots forms of knowledge production based in community interests, enacted through everyday interactions and formal classes and workshops.

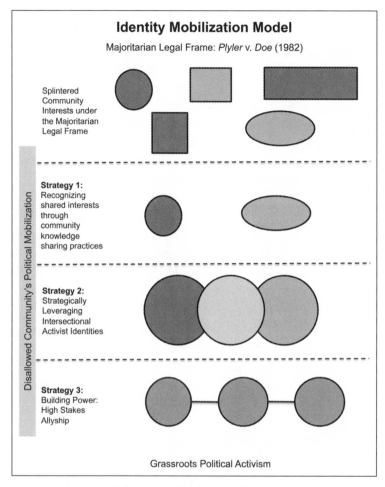

Figure 1.1. Identity Mobilization Model developed by Kevin Escudero

Rooted in a Freirian framework of popular education, critical race in education scholars' theorization of the importance of reconceptualizing informal knowledge-sharing mechanisms, and social movement scholarship on consciousness-raising, community knowledge–sharing practices combine these approaches as part of broader efforts among activists to facilitate raising one another's political and oppositional consciousness.[24] This occurs by activists educating one another about the important political histories pertaining to the movement's overall cause in an interpersonal and horizontal (i.e., nonhierarchical) manner.

Community meetings, conversations, and workshops and other less formal discussion-based spaces have largely been overlooked as key sites of knowledge-production in social movements. Rather than mimicking formal educational practices, these community-based methods of education and knowledge sharing are rooted in the personal and engage the personal as a means of critiquing the structural. Community knowledge–sharing practices are thus innovative, providing for a combined recognition of formal and informal knowledge production mechanisms in social movements and consider the central role that everyday, lived experience plays in this process.

In the contemporary immigrant rights movement, community knowledge–sharing strategies have consisted of activists coming together to share meals and spend time getting to know one another in other informal spaces, where participants share their personal experience as a means of educating one another about the multifaceted nature of undocumented immigrant identity. Doing so has allowed undocumented immigrant organizers to intentionally shift the discussion within community organizing spaces away from one that depicts undocumented immigration as solely a Latinx, and more specifically a Mexican, issue. Through these conversations and spaces created for informal interaction and dialogue, undocumented activists have emphasized the heterogeneous nature of undocumented immigrant experiences as it intersects with the plight of other communities.

A second strategy, the strategic leveraging of an intersectional movement identity, entails activists' sustained participation in other related social movement organizing spaces. As part of these efforts, activists holding an intersectional identity leverage their participation to assist in forging a dialogue between the two movements, drawing from their lived experiences as individuals affected by multiple social issues. Previous social movement scholarship has highlighted the importance of an intersectional identity in organizing.[25] Nevertheless, the role of strategy in this process remains an area that can be further explained and analyzed.[26] Also, as research on undocumented immigrant political activism has begun to consider undocumented immigrant activists' use of an intersectional identity, a model or framework for examining the processes through which this takes place in a strategic manner and across multiple social movement contexts does not yet exist.[27]

In the immigrant rights movement these efforts have primarily centered around undocumented immigrants' sustained participation in other
movement organizing spaces, in particular in LGBTQ and/or Asian American racial justice organizations. Drawing from their lived experiences,
through sustained involvement in these related movement spaces, undocumented immigrant activists have worked to introduce an analysis of
undocumented status into conversations on LGBTQ and Asian American
identity. In the process, immigrant rights organizers have not only sym-
bolically bridged these conversations but also built meaningful and lasting
relationships that can be further leveraged for future activist collaboration.

The third strategy, high-stakes allyship, refers to the participation of
allies who have a vested interest in the movement, though they do not
identify as "directly affected individuals." These individuals, similar to
directly affected movement participants, have a significant stake in the
welfare of directly affected movement participants given their embed-
dedness within the community on whose behalf they are fighting. Combining theories of high-risk activism and allyship, high-stakes allyship
offers a new way to read the inclusion of individuals with close ties to a
movement who hold both a personal and an ideological connection to
the issue at hand.

While social movement theorists' examination of high-risk activism
has emphasized the extended risk that activists take when organizing
for themselves or on behalf of members of a marginalized group, high-
stakes allyship underscores the connection between activists and allies
as part of a linked fate. This work builds on scholars' emphasis on the
importance of high-stakes activists' personal ties and connections to a
movement.[28] Additionally, though previous research on allyship has focused on the emotional reasons allies feel a particularly close affinity to a
movement's focal issue, how allies approach community building among
themselves, what movements can gain by viewing allies as a resource
to social movement organizing, and allies' navigation of their privilege
relative to other movement participants, high-stakes allyship is distinct
because it highlights the positionality of allies who have a unique personal connection to the issue.[29]

Sociologist Daniel Myers's work on political protest has importantly
examined the role of allies in social movement organizing; through this
work, he developed the concept of "insider-outsider" to explain how

allies "are members of the activist community, but not members of the beneficiary population that underlies the collective activist identity."[30] Yet, this distinction between ally and movement beneficiary is at times quite porous.[31] High-stakes allyship, as a theoretical concept, adds to the theorization of allyship in social movement scholarship by capturing the experiences of individuals who have a close relationship to a movement's overarching issue. While still rendered allies, these individuals have a unique connection to movement activists. Through the involvement of high-stakes allies, not solely as a potential resource but as an integral part of the movement, this strategy highlights these individuals' linked fate with directly affected movement participants as a motivating factor for their activism.[32]

In the immigrant rights movement the phrase "directly affected individual" refers to a person whose own ability to remain in the United States is directly affected by immigration laws and policies. Given the emergence of research highlighting the effects of undocumented status on family members—US citizen and legal permanent residents—high-stakes allyship also helps capture the effect of closely related movement participants who are not "directly affected individuals" but still experience the resonant effects of undocumented status.[33] This type of political participation is closely related to, but not quite the same as, the participation of a formerly undocumented individual who undergoes a shift from being a "directly affected individual" to someone with "citizenship privilege," as discussed in chapter 4.

Taken together, these strategies explain how activists in the immigrant rights movement—Asian undocumented, undocuqueer, and formerly undocumented individuals—engage their multiple social identities to work toward the development of an intersectional movement identity. Through the cultivation of coalitions with members of similarly situated groups, activists strategically deploy this intersectional identity as a means of counteracting the limitations they face when taking part in political activism as individuals who are not formally recognized as able to make rights claims in the first place. Rights claims in this context relate to formal political representation and the ability to engage in political activism without the fear and/or threat of deportation/removal from the United States. Needing to establish their presence as political actors who must be taken seriously and must have the ability to influence mainstream politics, activists have importantly emphasized their similarity, not necessarily to everyday Americans but to members of other similarly situated groups who also experience discrimination and marginalization on the basis of their identities. Through the cultivation of an intersectional movement identity, undocumented immigrant organizers have become well positioned to build bridges with other marginalized communities and expand their base of groups with connections to the issue of undocumented immigrant rights. This has led to a successful campaign to secure increased rights and political recognition at both the federal and the subfederal level.

Implications for Theories of Identity and Strategy in Social Movement Scholarship

Despite their exclusion from "formal" political mechanisms, undocumented immigrant youth have distinguished themselves as a key force in US politics. Their activism, analyzed through the lens of the Identity Mobilization Model, is instructive not only for future social movement participants but also for broadening an understanding of identity and its strategic use within social movement theory. Bringing together various strands of research in social movement scholarship on intersectional identity, coalition building, and strategy, this model builds from and contributes to a growing set of discussions regarding the political implications of "new social movements" in the contemporary period.

Describing activists' cultivation of an intersectional movement identity, sociologists Jennifer Chun, George Lipsitz, and Young Shin have highlighted the importance of an intersectional approach to identity within social movement research as it provides a means for examining a convergence of different identities, one that is deployable to assist in the formation of broad coalitions.[34] In a similar vein, the Identity Mobilization Model builds on this work and extends it to provide micro- and macro-level approaches to examining the processes through which such efforts to move from the individual to the collective, and ultimately to the structural, occur and do so in a manner that takes into account the stigmatized identity of the community engaging in such activism.

Regarding the importance of strategy in activists' use of identity in social movement activism, Mary Bernstein and Kristine Olsen explain the need to consider the role of strategy and connecting its use to the formation of an overarching collective identity of the movement: "Expressions of identity can be deployed at the collective level as a political strategy, which can be aimed at cultural and/or political goals [and] identity deployment can be examined at both the individual and collective level along a continuum from education to critique."[35] This work builds on Bernstein's earlier work on the three analytic dimensions of identity: identity for empowerment, identity as goal, and identity as strategy.[36] These varying uses of identity and the multiple levels at which it operates are taken into account in the model through the strategies that activists utilize when engaging in its use.

Bridging these two areas—identity and strategy—Anna Carastathis's work calls for scholars to recognize the role of intersectional identity in cultivating meaningful and productive coalitions in a social movement context.[37] Similar to the coalitional promise of intersectionality identified by Roberts and Jesudason, which follows the goals of some of the original theorists of an intersectional framework, this model engages in an analysis of the mechanisms and processes through which such coalition-building efforts occur.[38]

In addition to these discussions, social movement scholars have flagged the importance of a reoccurring set of questions for identity-based movements. Joshua Gamson, who has examined the role of identity in queer activism, termed this issue the "queer dilemma." According to Gamson, this dilemma consists of "a fundamental quandary: In the contemporary American political environment, clear identity categories are both necessary and dangerous distortions, and moves to both fix and unfix them are reasonable."[39] This dual role that identities play, especially in a social movement context, concerns the creation of categories that can, in turn, be utilized for political mobilization and then, through that mobilization process, can be deconstructed and critiqued. Elaborating on this concept, Gamson explains: "The destabilization of collective identity itself is a goal and accomplishment of movement action."[40] As the Identity Mobilization Model and the narratives of activists in the contemporary immigrant rights movement demonstrate, activists' efforts to develop a more inclusive approach to the creation of an undocumented immigrant identity may at times lead to the privileging of a certain subset of undocumented youth in the movement—those who have been able to attend college and who migrated to the United States at a very early age. Leading scholars in the field have pointed to the importance of analyzing the relationship between undocumented youth—members of the 1.5 generation—and members of the first generation, as well as the important implications that membership in these two generations has on political organizing.[41] So, too, have undocumented immigrant youth activists consciously worked to bridge this divide and to work alongside all members of the undocumented immigrant community. These efforts to broaden the scope of who is included in organizing decisions have also found their way into the use of an intersectional identity for conceptualizing members of the community as depicted in the Identity Mobilization Model. From Gamson's argument regarding the circular notion of identity to expand, but also from the destabilization that occurs, it would follow that the porous and ambiguous nature of undocumented immigrant identity would lead to a declining significance in the movement's ability to form a collective base. Yet, as the following chapters and the Identity Mobilization Model demonstrate, rather than this occurring, activists are instead able to broaden the issue to one that others—members of similarly situated marginalized groups—have an investment in supporting.

By delineating the specific strategies that undocumented immigrant activists have utilized to counteract the effects of what scholars have termed "migrant illegality," or the daily, lived experience of continually being subject to the threat of deportation, the Identity Mobilization Model contributes to the theorization of an intersectional methodological approach that acknowledges the framework's foundation in analyzing black women's subjectivities and demonstrates its relevance to the experiences of other multiply marginalized communities.[42] This work also seeks to examine these processes on a broader level, leading to a demonstration of the importance and necessity of applying these theoretical frameworks across social movement contexts to provide additional empirical evidence for their validity in exploring social movement phenomena.

A Multisited Ethnographic Approach: San Francisco, Chicago, and New York City

The three cities in which I conducted fieldwork for this book—San Francisco, Chicago, and New York—were selected on the basis of their placement in different regions of the US (West Coast, Midwest, and East Coast), their roles as historic destinations for documented and undocumented immigrant communities alike, and their histories as sites of high levels of immigrant political engagement and activism. In this process I sought to highlight the ways that the formation of Asian undocumented, undocuqueer, and formerly undocumented subgroups within the contemporary immigrant rights movement are indicative of a movement-wide phenomenon, one that has unfolded in parallel ways across similar sites: global urban immigrant cities.

In his frequently cited article theorizing the concept of a multisited ethnographic approach, anthropologist George Marcus highlights the utility of such a method in illuminating the inner workings of the world system or the "local," "global," "lifeworld," and "system."[43] Pointing to the field's transnational turn, David Fitzgerald has demonstrated the applicability of a multisited ethnographic approach to immigration scholarship in the social sciences, in particular looking at community formation, culture, and values across national borders. In this work, however, Fitzgerald also notes the potential role of intranational comparison of immigrant communities' experiences in revealing the "political quality of international migration and suggests the commonalities and differences with domestic urbanization."[44] This book takes up Fitzgerald's call for the use of a multisited ethnographic approach to examine variation among undocumented immigrant youth activists and the relationship of this variation to the formation of the movement's strategies and tactics.

Previous research on undocumented immigrant youth activism has underscored the central role of key urban immigrant gateways in facilitating immigrant political participation. As foundational immigration scholars writing on undocumented immigrant youth activism have noted, Los Angeles and the greater Southern California region have shaped the trajectory of the national immigrant rights movement.[45] This foundational work has also examined the influence of other global cities, including Chicago and Boston.[46] In this book, I demonstrate how examining undocumented immigrant political mobilization through the use of a multisited ethnographic approach can facilitate a more contextualized understanding of how national trends are reflected across different activist sites and locales.

As scholars Walter Nicholls and Justus Uitermark have noted, cities and their environments can play a significant role in promoting or inhibiting social movement participation. Elaborating on this point, they write: "Some cities provide rich environments for seeds for resistance to grow into robust mobilizations but activists in many cities do not always connect with others and develop productive political relations. Many factors impede such relations. Some advocacy organizations may simply have sufficient resources of their own and may not need to develop partnerships with other organizations in their environment. Others may find themselves competing for the same recruits and sources of financing, which can exacerbate ideological and strategic conflicts. And still others may face institutional and discursive constraints imposed by local governance regimes."[47] Given the potential of cities and their role in facilitating political mobilization, I would like to describe the similarities between the three cities chosen for this book that facilitated my ability to focus on the intersectional group identities that formed across these sites.

San Francisco, Chicago, and New York City are all relatively large cities in terms of overall population, each ranking within the top fifteen largest cities nationally, with Chicago and New York City ranking in the top three.[48] These cities have traditionally served as key gateways for immigrants from all backgrounds entering the United States, including those with and without legal status. As depicted in table 1.1, in the counties where I conducted fieldwork for this book, undocumented immigrants constituted between 17 and 28 percent of the county's foreignborn population. These percentages were close to the national average of the foreign-born population that is undocumented: 26 percent.

Additionally, all three cities are self-proclaimed sanctuary cities, meaning that their leadership has pledged not to collaborate with federal agencies to actively deport undocumented immigrants, though this may be enacted differently across each locale.[49] As sanctuary cities, they have also proactively worked to promote inclusive laws and policies to assist undocumented residents as they navigate daily life by providing munici-

TABLE 1.1. Foreign-Born and Unauthorized Populations, as Share of Total Population, in San Francisco, Chicago, and New York City

	Total Population[a]	Foreign-Born[b]		Unauthorized Population[c]		
		Estimate	Percent of Total Population	Estimate	Percent of Foreign-Born	Percent of Total Population
United States	318,558,000	42,914,000	13	11,300,000	26	3.5
Chicago Area						
Cook County	5,228,000	1,102,000	21	307,000	28	5.9
DuPage County	931,000	175,000	19	37,000	21	4.0
New York City Area						
Bronx County	1,437,000	502,000	35	120,000	24	8.4
Kings County	2,607,000	971,000	37	191,000	20	7.3
New York County	1,635,000	472,000	29	90,000	19	5.5
Queens County	2,310,000	1,098,000	48	256,000	23	11.1
Richmond County	473,000	104,000	22	n.a.[d]	n.a.	n.a.
San Francisco Bay Area						
Alameda County	1,605,000	509,000	32	109,000	21	6.8
Contra Costa County	1,108,000	270,000	24	69,000	26	6.2
San Francisco County	850,000	297,000	35	49,000	17	5.8
San Mateo County	755,000	261,000	35	58,000	22	7.7

a 2012–2016 American Community Survey 5-Year Estimates: Total Population Figures rounded to nearest 1,000s.
b 2012–2016 American Community Survey 5-Year Estimates: Nativity in the United States Figures rounded to nearest 1,000s.
c Migration Policy Institute: Estimate based on the Migration Policy Institute's analysis of US Census Bureau data from the pooled 2012–16 American Community Survey and the 2008 Survey of Income and Program Participation, drawing on a methodology developed in consultation with James Bachmeier of Temple University and Jennifer Van Hook of Pennsylvania State University, Population Research Institute. www.migrationpolicy.org.
d Estimate not available because the number of sample cases is too small.

pal identification cards, which, within the city limits and at certain city offices and vendors, function the same as any other government-issued piece of identification.[50] These three cities are home to colleges and universities that have, as the result of student activism and organizing, developed stronger measures to support and be inclusive of undocumented immigrant students. The increased educational support, in turn, has led to greater politicization of undocumented students and future social movement organizers.[51] Public colleges and universities in San Francisco, Chicago, and New York City have in recent years developed programs to assist immigrant youth, in particular undocumented youth, in accessing the US higher education system. Some private institutions in these regions have also undertaken efforts to support undocumented students, but not on the same scale as the public universities. California, Illinois, and New York, the states in which these cities are located, have passed legislation allowing certain undocumented students to pay in-state or resident tuition when attending a public college or university (table 1.2). These state-level laws have helped create an environment in which educational institutions in these cities can continue to innovate and provide additional resources and support systems for members of this student population. Alongside this vast array of colleges and universities that offer growing support for undocumented students, regionally based nonprofits and grassroots community-based organizations in these cities have provided an important outlet for immigrant residents to voice their concerns on topics such as wage theft, police racial profiling, and unequal access to the pursuit of higher education and to translate these grievances into concrete legal and policy victories. Many of these grassroots community-based organization have been led and supported by undocumented immigrants. Though some of these groups began with the support of formal nonprofit organizations, a few have since broken off to establish their own autonomous organizations.

Thus, these cities—San Francisco, Chicago, and New York—have relatively congruous legal and political contexts that are friendly and welcoming to immigrants, including undocumented immigrants. More specifically, undocumented immigrant youth's location in global immigrant cities and their unique legal positioning have resulted in a growing, ambitious movement of youth activists fighting nationally for increased rights for all immigrant community members. As social science scholars have noted, cities and other subfederal entities provide a critical lens for examining the role of space and place in facilitating the integration and incorporation of immigrants; in fact, this scholarship has highlighted the central role of place in facilitating of a global democratic struggle for rights and increased representation.[52] For undocumented immigrants, individuals who have been denied legal recognition in their host society, cities and local urban spaces have proved to be a key site for the construction of a piecemeal version of citizenship for individuals who experience the structural and legal exclusionary practices on a daily basis. Relatedly, as became clear from the research I conducted for this book,

TABLE 1.2. Major State Legislation Passed in California, Illinois, and New York Impacting Undocumented Students' Access to Public Higher Education (2001–2019)

State	Name of Legislative Bill	Year Passed	Provisions
California	Assembly Bill 540 (AB 540)	2001	Provides qualified undocumented students with in-state tuition and state-funded financial aid Eligibility requirements:
	Assembly Bill 130 (AB 130)	2011	• Must have attended a California high school for at least three academic years
	Assembly Bill 131 (AB 131)	2011	• Must have graduated from a California high school, attained a GED, or received a passing mark on the California High School Proficiency Exam (CHSPE) • Must enroll at an accredited institution of public higher education in California • If required by the individual institution, must file or plan to file an affidavit stating that the student will apply for legal residency as soon as possible
Illinois	Public Act 093-007 (HB 0060), In-State Tuition	2003	Provides undocumented students with in-state tuition and privately funded scholarships Eligibility requirements: • Resided with his or her parent or guardian while attending a public or private high school in Illinois
	Public Act 097-0233 (SB 2185), Illinois DREAM Act	2011	• Graduated from a public or private high school or received the equivalent of a high school diploma in Illinois • Attended school in Illinois for at least three years as of the date of graduating from high school or receiving the equivalent of a high school diploma • Registers as an entering student in the university not earlier than the 2003 fall semester • Provides the university with an affidavit stating that the individual will file an application to become a permanent resident of the United States at the earliest opportunity the individual is eligible to do so
New York	9612-A (SB 7784)	2002	Provides in-state tuition to eligible undocumented students Eligibility requirements: • Attended at least two years of high school in New York • Graduated from a New York high school or received a GED • Apply for attendance at an institution within five years of receiving a diploma • Show proof of residence • File affidavit declaring that you will file for legal status when able
	SB S1250	2019	Allows undocumented students to qualify for state aid for higher education and for undocumented families to enroll in the New York College Tuition Savings Program Eligibility requirements: • Attended at least two years of high school in New York • Graduated from a New York high school or received a GED • Applied for attendance at an undergraduate institution where the award would be applied within five years of receiving a New York State high school diploma or equivalent GED • Eligible for in-state tuition at the State University of New York, the City University of New York, or New York State community college • Provide the university with an affidavit stating that the individual will file an application to become a permanent resident of the United States at the earliest opportunity the individual is eligible to do so

Source: uLEAD network (https://uleadnet.org); New York State Senate (https://legislation.nystate.gov).

there is a continued value in examining the interaction between federal and subfederal government entities as they shape the context in which immigrant rights organizing takes place.

An Inclusive Approach to Undocumented Immigrant Identity: Asian Undocumented, Undocuqueer, and Formerly Undocumented Activist Experiences

In conducting research for this book and developing the Identity Mobilization Model, I focused on the participation of three groups of activists within the contemporary immigrant rights movement. As sociological research on social movement activism has pointed out, identity plays a key role in shaping the ways individuals choose to take part in a social movement and the ways they participate once they have decided to become involved. More specifically, this research demonstrates the role of collective identity in facilitating the cultivation of a group consciousness and the mobilization around a particular set of shared goals and values.[53] Yet scholarship on identity and social movements has also acknowledged the difficulties in cultivating such an overarching identity and the importance of examining intragroup variation.[54] Taking a cue from this work, I focus on three subgroups within the undocumented immigrant community to demonstrate how multiple groups within the community, each in its own way, have taken up the development of a nuanced, multifaceted approach to undocumented immigrant identity. I now outline the contours of these groups' activist involvement and cultivation of an intersectional movement identity.

Asian Undocumented Activists at the Nexus of Historical and Contemporary Migration Narratives

Asian undocumented immigrants' participation in contemporary immigrant rights activism draws on both a historical legacy of Asian undocumented migration and present-day coalition-building efforts between Asian and Latinx undocumented immigrant activists. These historical narratives, however, stand in stark contrast to contemporary understandings of Asian immigrants, who are viewed in the public imaginary as hardworking, highly skilled immigrants largely from East

Asian and South Asian countries. This uncontextualized depiction of Asian immigration has been further drawn upon by individuals seeking to reproduce the model minority myth, juxtaposed with the plight of Latinx migrants. In this process, Latinx migrants are often depicted as constituting the quintessential undocumented immigrant community, crossing the border with little regard for US immigration laws and policies and not "waiting their turn in line."[55]

Historical Roots: The Development of Immigration Policing through Racial Exclusion and the Model Minority Myth

Asian undocumented immigrants were not only the first undocumented immigrants to the United States but also the first community on which the federal government honed its ability to surveil and deport immigrant community members.[56] Moreover, this community was the first to be excluded and to be subjected to the newly developed machinery of the US government. Such efforts have since evolved into what sociologist Tanya Golash-Boza has referred to as a multifaceted "immigration industrial complex," which can be understood as "the public and private sector interests in the criminalization of undocumented migration, immigration law enforcement and the promotion of 'anti-illegal' rhetoric."[57] As historian Mae Ngai has demonstrated, this immigration industrial complex was built upon and (re)produced an underlying racial logic that constructed Asian and Latin American migrants as "illegal" and their European counterparts as assimilable into the US body politic.[58] This unique place that Asian undocumented immigrants occupy in the historical narrative has been underemphasized and overlooked by individuals seeking to praise Asian Americans as the model minority.

Racial bars to migration during the Chinese exclusion era (1882–1943) and the subsequent Gentlemen's Agreement between the United States and Japan (1907) forced many Asian migrants to find alternative routes to enter the country. As historian Robert Chao Romero explains, some of these alternative routes entailed Asian immigrant smuggling into the United States via Latin America—what he terms "transnational commercial orbits."[59] Those who did not enter through Latin America resorted to assuming the identities of others and using false documents to enter the United States, a tactic commonly known as the "paper sons and paper daughters scheme."[60]

Much of this historical narrative has been obscured, and the differences between Asian and Latinx undocumented immigrants have been reinforced through the notion of the model minority myth. Historian Ellen Wu documents how the model minority paradigm has contributed to this erasure. In her book *The Model Minority Myth*, Wu explains how Asians and Asian Americans were rendered as "a racial group distinct from the majority, politically nonthreatening, and *definitively not-black*."[61] The shift in Asian Americans' earlier positioning as unassimilable into the nation-state and racially undesirable subjects to exceptional citizens, however, did not occur overnight or without intervention of state actors. Rather, it was part of a larger project to place the voices of some communities of color in opposition to others vis-à-vis a cultural deficit framework. By emphasizing the importance of this historical narrative and placing it in conversation with contemporary narratives, Asian undocumented migration activists have steadfastly worked to contest these divisive logics and nuance the narrative regarding undocumented immigrant history in the United States.

Forging a New Narrative: Contemporary Asian Undocumented Immigrant Activist Efforts

Alongside efforts to nuance the historical narrative, Asian undocumented immigrants have also incorporated these historical narratives into contemporary discussions of undocumented immigrant political activism. With limited scholarly writings on the experiences of Asian undocumented immigrants and a growing but nascent Asian undocumented contingent within the immigrant rights movement, these efforts have consisted primarily of scholarly interventions and the publication of community-based resources showcasing the importance of an intersectional Asian undocumented immigrant perspective.

Of the 11.2 million undocumented immigrants currently residing in the United States, approximately 13 percent are estimated to be from Asia, with substantial representation of Korean and Filipino youth.[62] Despite Asian undocumented youth's numerical representation within the overall undocumented population, few scholarly writings have addressed their participation in the contemporary immigrant rights movement.[63] Further research is therefore needed to examine the experiences of this population, including South Asian, East Asian, and Southeast Asian immigrant youth.[64]

Other than the important, but few, scholarly studies of Asian undocumented communities, much of the narrative about this community has come directly from activists. These activist-rooted studies have emphasized not only increasing the visibility of these community members' narratives but also connecting Asian and Latinx undocumented experiences as part of the construction of an overarching undocumented immigrant identity. One example of community-initiated scholarship is the edited volume *Undocumented and Unafraid: Tam Tran, Cynthia Felix and the Immigrant Youth Movement*. This book, which discusses the legacy of interracial solidarity and coalition building within the undocumented youth movement, commemorates the lives of two undocumented youth activists, one of them Vietnamese American and the other Mexican American, who were tragically killed in a car accident.[65] Taking the lead from activists, Asian American nonprofit organizations have also begun to focus on the challenges facing undocumented youth by organizing national speaking tours and other events to raise awareness that "we too are undocumented."[66] These campaigns have taken multiple forms: protests, media campaigns, and storytelling events.

Undocuqueer: At the Nexus of Undocumented and Queer Immigrant Identities

Referring to the intersection of queer and undocumented immigrant identities, the term "undocuqueer" is rooted in social movement activists' efforts to name and theorize the far-reaching effects of immigration laws in multiple contexts and for members of multiply marginalized communities, in this case the queer community. Undocuqueer identity has been theorized by scholars in multiple fields, including queer studies, communication studies, and sociology.[67] Combining academic discussions of the term "undocuqueer" with community-based and activist articulations, I operationalize the term as referring to the intersectional experience of identifying as both queer and undocumented.

The narratives of two undocuqueer activists in particular—Nico and Jorge—highlight the term's community-based origins and its development out of the need to create an inclusive term that fully captures the experiences of being both queer and undocumented. In a 2012 YouTube post, Nico, an undocuqueer-identified activist from the greater Chicago region, explained how undocuqueer individuals see their identities as unique in comparison to other queer and undocumented organizers and the importance of undocuqueer individuals' needs within the broader immigrant rights movement. Nico explained:

> For me personally . . . having to live on my own. . . . put me into a place where I had to struggle . . . and it was funny because you have to come out as a queer person and as [an] undocumented [person]. Seeing that in our community, there's a lot of stigma with being queer and even when there have been conferences or gatherings, you always see people saying negative things about being queer. And you know, to us, it has been really important to talk about it and put it out there that it's not right. And having that time to talk about being queer and the importance of that.[68]

As Nico's comments illustrate, it is important to name the specific forms of marginalization that undocuqueer community members faced and how it differs from the experiences of their queer and undocumented counterparts. This unique subject position, as Nico explained, helped contribute to a shared mode of navigating other movement organizing spaces. Jorge, a self-identified undocuqueer organizer from the greater Los Angeles region, echoed Nico's sentiments in terms of the unique experiences of undocuqueer movement participants and further emphasized the underrepresentation of queer narratives in the immigrant rights movement. In another YouTube video, Jorge explained:

> You know at times when I walked into a meeting or went into a rally, I was like today I'm wearing my undocumented hat only, but not my queer hat. I could point out that there were other gay folks or queer folks in the room, but they were not sharing their stories . . . but I found it very difficult and it was really painful. . . . I came to the realization that . . . I could

not negotiate, that I had to be both every time in front of everyone at every rally, at every press conference, at every meeting [as an undocuqueer activist].[69]

Rather than referring to having to shift between identities or to mask one identity to foreground the other, Jorge's remarks highlight the importance and liberation of simultaneously embracing one's queer and undocumented identities. Moreover, through the activism of undocuqueer organizers such as Nico and Jorge, the cultivation of a nuanced theorization of undocuqueer identity has been led by those individuals who inhabit this particular intersectional lived experience. Given this undocuqueer leadership in the broader immigrant rights movement and in carving out a space for discussions of their own intersectional identity, the immigrant rights community has worked to craft a nuanced, complex movement identity that goes beyond centralizing an already stigmatized identity—undocumented immigrant status—toward one that affirms difference as a means of achieving community empowerment. These efforts have also worked to recenter the importance of sexuality in contemporary discussions of migrant rights, demonstrated by the innovative chant "Undocumented and Unafraid, Queer and Unashamed," often heard at rallies and movement events today.[70]

While "undocuqueer" is understood as a term developed by and for queer and undocumented community members, this community's lived experiences have also been analyzed by social science research in relation to undocumented immigrant youth's participation in social movement activism. As interdisciplinary scholarship on this topic has noted, a key area of overlap between the two communities' experiences is the "coming-out" process, or the act by which individuals disclose their identities to those in their communities.[71] Legal scholar Rose Cuison Villazor adds to this discussion by examining the construction of the closet for queer-identified people and the undocumented closet for immigrant community members, as well as the overlap between the two for undocuqueer-identified individuals.[72] Articulating a framework for understanding the relationship between queer and migrant justice movement paradigms, communications studies scholar Karma Chavez introduces the notion of a "queer migration politics." According to Chavez, a queer migration politics can be understood as an "examin[ation of the] instances where migration politics and queer politics meet in ways that challenge this type of inclusionary strategy and shift the political focus to other sites of activism."[73] This framework, as Chavez explains, illuminates the overlapping nature of these two paradigms and the ways that they reinforce the status quo through calls for inclusion and membership but also go beyond normative frameworks by advancing more radical framings of queerness and immigrant identity.

Building on these community-based and scholarly analyses of undocuqueer identity and its relationship to social movement activism, this book utilizes the Identity Mobilization Model framework to place this particular form of intersectional activism in conversations with other intersectional movement constituencies: Asian undocumented and formerly undocumented movement participants.

Formerly Undocumented Immigrant Activists' Experiences

The third group of individuals whose experiences this book discusses—formerly undocumented immigrant activists—are a uniquely situated community in that while its members are no longer individually affected by being undocumented, they have very deep connections to movement organizing spaces and leaders in those spaces. Of the formerly undocumented immigrant activists I interviewed, the majority identified as formerly undocumented immigrant women of color who adjusted their immigration status through marriage to a US citizen spouse. Thus, my theorization of formerly undocumented immigrants' experiences draws from the foundational work of sociologists who have articulated the importance of gender and race as forming a coconstitutive framework for examining immigrant identity.

The Use of a Gendered Lens for Analyzing the Social Movement Participation of Formerly Undocumented Activists

Leading social science immigration scholars have highlighted the central importance of gender as an important yet understudied aspect of the migration process.[74] This rich area of research has considered immigrant women's agency in the migration process, women's decision to leave their home countries, transnational parenting and caring practices, violence targeting immigrant mothers and women, and the gendered nature of the US naturalization process.[75] Some key scholarship has also noted the deportation regime's targeting of undocumented immigrant men and the migration of queer immigrant men.[76] More recently, work in the field has focused on the intersection of gendered migration experiences and the phenomenon of migrant illegality, particularly regarding opportunities for undocumented individuals to adjust their immigration status; undocumented immigrants' dating, marriage, and parenting experiences; and the family-level effects of undocumented status for those in marriages with US citizen spouses.[77] Yet, as Katherine Donato, Laura Enriquez, and Cheryl Llewellyn note in their introduction to a special issue of *American Behavioral Scientist* examining the gendered nature of migrant illegality, further discussion is needed not only on women's immigration narratives but on how these experiences intersect with one's legal status.[78] Contributing to this rich area of scholarship, my research on formerly undocumented immigrant women's experiences examines the impact of a shift in legal status on these women's understanding of their positionality in the movement. I analyze how these formerly undocumented immigrant women draw upon their multiple social identities to negotiate their continued participation in the immigrant rights movement. As a result, I argue that these women take part in emotional labor, mentorship, and care work that aim to support younger generations of undocumented movement organizers. Additionally, by centering the experiences of these community members, I aim to highlight the importance of shifts in legal status to nuance the category of "undocumented immigrant" and "directly affected individual" and to illuminate the strategic choices of these activists as an important aspect of this intersectional experience and relationship to other intersectional subgroups within the immigrant rights movement.

Marriage as a Path to Adjusting One's Immigration Status

Among the formerly undocumented activists I interviewed, the majority adjusted their status through marriage to a US citizen. While this is not the only route available to undocumented immigrants seeking to adjust their immigration status—other options include employer sponsorship, a U visa or T visa, or asylum/refugee status—it was the primary route utilized by the individuals' whose experiences I describe.

As anthropologist Ruth Gomberg-Muñoz explains, adjustment of status through marriage primarily takes place through one of two potential routes: (1) adjustment of status under Section 245(a) of the Immigration and Nationality Act or (2) consular processing. The main distinction between the two routes is the mode through which the individual entered the United States.[79] An undocumented person who entered the country without a temporary visa, or, as immigration scholars often call "with inspection," is eligible to pursue adjustment of status under Section 245(a); otherwise, consular processing is often the route pursued. Adjustment under Section 245(a) entails having a US citizen spouse, parent, or child older than twenty-one file a petition on behalf of the undocumented individual.[80] In comparison, consular processing primarily entails applying for a visa from within the United States, then leaving the United States and traveling to a consulate to interview for and receive a visa to reenter the country. Individuals who have been undocumented in the United States for more than 180 days must also apply for a hardship waiver to prevent the three- and ten-year bars from being incurred.[81]

Work conducted by Gomberg-Muñoz and Chicana/o studies scholar Lucia Leon has pointed to the shift experienced by undocumented individuals as they navigate the marriage-based legislation process. Leon highlights the various circumstances under which undocumented immigrants who marry US citizens decide to pursue marriage-based adjustment of their immigration status. Explaining the added layer of complexity that immigrant legal status adds to discussions of marriage for undocumented young adults, Leon writes, "Much like their U.S.-born counterparts, undocumented young adults enter romantic relationships and contemplate the next steps in their relationships—mainly [becoming engaged] and marriage. However, for undocumented young adults their decisions to get engaged and to marry are mediated by a complex negotiation between their personal decisions about their relationships, the social/cultural expectations of marriage, and the role of their marriage as the medium for a legalization pathway and the obtainment of their legal status."[82] Focusing on the Southern California context, Leon found that for some undocumented individuals, their decision to marry their US citizen partner was the result of a "convergence of 'love and papers'" and the gendered nature of the familial and partner expectations of their role in the marriage.[83] Building on this foundational work of scholars such as Gomberg-Muñoz and Leon, this book examines the shift from being an undocumented immigrant to obtaining legal status in relation to these individuals' continued participation and involvement in social movement activism.

Of the formerly undocumented immigrant activists interviewed for this book, I specifically chose to focus on formerly undocumented women. These formerly undocumented women activists hailed primarily from San Francisco and Chicago. These women described meeting their spouses in a variety of contexts, such as college and activist spaces, although some met their spouses through extended friend networks. These women's spouses often hailed from immigrant families themselves, and, as participants relayed to me during our interviews, it was often their spouses who, having seen firsthand the impact of undocumented status on their immediate and extended family members' lives, urged these undocumented women to consider marriage as a potential path to adjusting their immigration status. Given that all formerly undocumented individuals who participated in my fieldwork remained active in immigrant rights movement organizing spaces, I often met them as they were undergoing the process of adjusting their immigration status and negotiating their future role in movement activism. Negotiating in this sense refers to these individuals' decisions about whether or not to continue their activism and, if so, in what form.

Conclusion

Outlining *Organizing While Undocumented*'s overarching theoretical framework—the Identity Mobilization Model—and providing additional context to understand the scope of the community with which I worked in conducting research for this book, this chapter serves as a road map of sorts for readers before they make their way through the subsequent fieldwork-based chapters. Each of the later chapters focuses on one subgroup and explores how that subgroup takes up the three strategies of the Identity Mobilization Model. While the following chapters demonstrate the micro-level processes through which activists "on the ground" connected their efforts to shifting power relations and reworking institutionalized structures leading to the marginalization of multiple communities, this chapter has described the circumstances and preconditions that made such activism possible.

2

Asian and Undocumented

Illuminating a Silenced Past Embedded within
Contemporary Narratives

Speaking at a 2011 immigrant rights rally in downtown Chicago, Karla, a self-identified Asian undocumented immigrant organizer, addressed the crowd that had gathered the morning of the event. In her remarks Karla highlighted the invisibility of Asian undocumented immigrant narratives in the greater immigrant rights movement and the importance of having Asian undocumented youth, similar to their Latinx counterparts, publicly acknowledge the impact of undocumented migration on their own communities. She shared, "To all the DREAMers out there in my community, to all the young people hiding out in your bedrooms, wishing with all your heart that something would change, that this country would finally recognize *you* as an American. You can't wish for change nor can you go at it alone. In the Asian American community we don't talk openly about being undocumented in fear of bringing shame to our families and ourselves. But refusing to address a problem that plagues us, too, doesn't make it go away."[1] As Karla's remarks pointed out, while undocumented immigration may be conceived of in the public imaginary as pertaining primarily to the case of Latinx individuals, concerns regarding immigrant legal status are also highly relevant to the lives of Asian immigrant community members. The fear and shame associated with one's undocumented status in the Asian immigrant community, which Karla alluded to, have led not only to the isolation of Asian undocumented activists but also to a hesitancy to publicly disclose one's immigration status to other non-Asian undocumented individuals and Asian immigrant community members. Yet, rather than allowing this fear and hesitancy to prevent Asian undocumented activists from participating in immigrant rights activism, Karla offers a call to participate and to "address a problem" to bring about tangible solutions to Asian undocumented immigrants' marginalization within the broader narrative of undocumented immigrant organizing in the United States today. As the narratives of movement participants in this chapter demonstrate, the intersection of an Asian and undocumented identity has served as a highly generative space for intersectional social movement activism.

In their organizing, Asian undocumented activists have emphasized a finding that Asian American studies scholars, particularly Asian American historians, have underscored in their scholarship: Asian immigrants were the first undocumented immigrant community in the United Sates.[2] Their inadmissibility to the United States began with the federal government's passage of the Chinese Exclusion Act in 1882 and related legislation pertaining to the entry of other Asian immigrants.[3] The exclusion period in turn led prospective Asian immigrants to find alternate routes to enter the United States, many traveling through Latin American nations and using false documents.[4] While post-1965 Asian immigration to the US led to increased numbers of East Asian immigrants entering the country with visas or through family reunification policies, Asian undocumented immigration, a pattern that initially began in the middle to late 1800s, also continued during this period. Current activists' efforts have thus highlighted the central role of Asian immigrants in the development of US immigration policies, leading to the creation of the "illegal alien," and the myriad of ways that activists have worked to exert rights and claim membership despite the continued stigma of illegality.[5]

These efforts can be read as an enactment of what historian Natalia Molina describes as racial scripts. Explaining how the concept functions, Molina writes:

> I coin the term *racial scripts* to highlight the ways in which the lives of racialized groups are linked across time and space and thereby affect one another, even when they do not directly cross paths. . . . A racial scripts approach pulls the lens back so that we can see different racial projects operating at the same time, affecting different groups simultaneously. . . . [S]tudying racial scripts will help us see connections between groups . . . [and] racialized groups put forth their own scripts, *counterscripts* that offer alternatives . . . directly challeng[ing] the dominant racial scripts.[6]

By bringing the historical racialization of Asian Americans into conversation with contemporary forms of racialization and then making comparisons across the contemporary racialization of Asian and Latinx undocumented communities, these Asian undocumented organizers are enacting precisely what Molina articulates. These two groups, Asian and Latinx undocumented communities, are linked by a shared experience of US government oppression, persecution, and marginalization, even if not during the same time periods. In the contemporary moment, however, these groups have experienced simultaneous forms of persecution despite the different historical origins of these forms of state-sanctioned marginalization. Working in a parallel manner, the federal government's surveillance of immigrant communities, in particular unauthorized immigrants, can be more fully understood by a linking of the past and present. This approach's recognition of a group's agency through the creation of a counternarrative underscores the need for academic approaches that illuminate the daily lived experiences of the marginalized communities whose perspectives have often been overlooked and/or obfuscated by traditional majoritarian narratives in the historical record.

This chapter examines how, by connecting the often overlooked historical narrative of Asian undocumented immigration with contemporary experiences of Asian undocumented immigrants, activists have marshaled their understanding of their communities' historical past to contextualize their contemporary use of an intersectional—Asian and undocumented—movement identity. In the process they have taken up the way that Asian Americans are rendered part of the "model minority" with the ability to "outperform" middle- and upper-class whites in terms of their hyperassimilation, highlighting the limitations and divisions that such a narrative perpetuates among Asian immigrant and Asian American community members.[7] Crafting a racial counterscript that imagines Asian undocumented immigrant communities alongside their Latinx undocumented peers, these organizers have worked to present a more nuanced context for understanding contemporary Asian migration in the present day.

Like the subsequent ethnographic chapters, this chapter begins with a brief discussion of the Identity Mobilization Model in practice, followed by a discussion of community-building, narrative-sharing practices that are aimed at subgroup and externally facing cohesion, the strategic use of pan-group activist spaces and subgroup-specific spaces of activism, and the production of high-stakes allyship. I then conclude with the broader implications of this subgroup's experiences for undocumented activism.

The Identity Mobilization Model in Practice

Consisting of a set of three interrelated yet not necessarily sequential strategies, the Identity Mobilization Model provides a framework for analyzing the strategic and intentional use of an intersectional identity by undocumented immigrant activists, as well as other similarly situated groups. Using this framework, one is able to examine the mechanisms through which Asian undocumented immigrant activists have successfully utilized their intersectional Asian and undocumented immigrant identities to cultivate alliances between the following groups: Asian immigrant and nonimmigrant communities and Asian and Latinx undocumented immigrant community members. A unique intersectional identity—the Asian undocumented immigrant experience—demonstrates the potential to examine the dual experiences of Asian American racialization and the marginalization that undocumented immigrants in the United States face on a daily basis.

Complex Storytelling Practices: The Use of Internally and Externally Focused Narratives to Build Community and Demonstrate the Importance of Linked Fate

As the narratives in this section demonstrate, community knowledge–sharing practices, or the knowledge-sharing mechanisms activists have utilized to communicate information, resulted in the heightened political and oppositional consciousness of potential movement participants. In the immigrant rights movement, storytelling—a tool that can be understood as a community knowledge–sharing practice—has served as a primary mechanism through which consciousness-raising has taken place and has functioned in a twofold manner. First, storytelling has been used to raise awareness internally among undocumented immigrant activists regarding the presence of Asian undocumented communities; second, it has functioned to promote a unified image of Asian and Latinx undocumented activists in external-facing movement spaces. Achieved through multiple approaches and avenues, these consciousness-raising efforts have broadened coalition-building initiatives to strengthen ties between Asian and Latinx and other subgroups within the immigrant rights movement.

Storytelling is a complex and often nonlinear process. As sociologist Francesca Polletta argues, storytelling is a process that, especially in the context of social movement activism, "comes with risks as well as benefits."[8] The utility of stories, Polletta continues, depends on their use and the subjectivity of the individual telling the story: "Stories are differentially intelligible, useful and authoritative depending on who tells them, when, for what purpose, and in what setting."[9] Embedded within these stories and the storytelling process are understandings of the law and the legal system and its role in shaping individuals' everyday lived experiences.[10] As the stories of Asian undocumented immigrant activists in this chapter demonstrate, these storytelling and narrative-sharing practices have largely taken the form of what social movement scholars have referred to as "movement repertoires," or frameworks and/or strategies that apply across various social movements and movement contexts.[11] A primary repertoire that activists have adopted in their work, also discussed in the following chapter, is that of "coming out," or disclosing one's identity as a member of a marginalized and/or socially stigmatized group. While this repertoire is often discussed in the context of LGBTQ activism, immigrant rights organizers' use of "coming out" points to its role in serving as a consciousness-raising tactic focused on reaching both internal and external movement audiences.

Storytelling and Narrative Sharing: Internally Focused

The cases of two Asian undocumented activists in particular, Henry and Anna, illustrate the two types of reception encountered by organizers who have used storytelling as an internally focused community knowledge–sharing practice. While Henry and others like him experienced an overwhelmingly positive reception by their undocumented immigrant peers as individuals who could potentially raise the profile of Asian undocumented immigrant movement participants, Anna and other activists were met with skepticism due to the hidden and often-underemphasized narrative of Asian undocumented immigrant experiences. The contrasting reception of these activists points to the excitement of non-Asian-identified undocumented immigrants in learning more about the experiences of this often hidden and less visible group within their own community, but also the fear and shame that many Asian undocumented individuals face, making them hesitant to disclose their status even to members of their own community. Storytelling and narrative-sharing practices in the context of Asian undocumented activists are related to the multiple audiences for these efforts. Internally, these audiences can be understood as other non-Asian undocumented movement participants, Asian immigrant peers with legal status in the United States, and Asian undocumented peers. Asian undocumented immigrants' unique positionality as both Asian and undocumented allows them to navigate these different yet inter-related spaces and intervene in the conversation, drawing on their own narratives to underscore the need for increased collaboration between group members.

Describing his experience of publicly coming out as an Asian undocumented immigrant, Henry, an undocumented Korean activist from the San Francisco Bay Area, detailed the multistep process he underwent when making that decision and in working to engage his peers as part of the process. As Henry explained, initially he focused his efforts internally, working to raise awareness among members of the immigrant rights movement in the community in which he grew up: "I shared my immigration status with the [community college] newspaper, and got really good, positive feedback. I then continued to publicize my story and gradually became a little more comfortable."[12] Starting with the context of his hometown and local college, Henry first tested the reactions he received from his peers regarding disclosure of his undocumented immigrant status. Given the extremely positive reception he experienced, Henry later continued sharing his story and doing so in an increasingly public manner. As a result, he decided to use the platform of social media to share his experience with a broader audience, namely, those within the national immigrant rights movement. He continued: "I even decided to release a YouTube [video] and created [a] personal webpage and blog. After that things kind of exploded in a way because nonprofit organizations were like 'wow—it's a Korean undocumented student actually coming out' and there were so many opportunities for me to do speaking engagements and do a lot of work around the DREAM Act and A.B. 540."[13] As Henry's comments demonstrate, he began with coming out as an Asian undocumented immigrant and later used this experience to position himself as an organizer within the immigrant rights movement. By identifying himself as an Asian undocumented organizer to his peers, he was able to embrace a fuller conception of his self-identity and serve as a role model and mentor for others.

Yet, Henry's experience coming out as an Asian undocumented organizer also had a secondary effect of bringing about feelings of isolation and loneliness as one of the few Asian, let alone Korean, undocumented students speaking out about their immigration status. Relatedly, the responsibility that Henry felt tasked with—representing his community, both the Asian and the undocumented immigrant community—and the call to educate immigrant rights organizers about how they could be more inclusive of Asian immigrant narratives in their work caused him to feel torn about his role in the movement. This confusion pertained to self-questioning regarding to whom he was to be held responsible or to whom he saw his work being accountable: members of the broader undocumented immigrant community, fellow Asian undocumented organizers, or both. Thus, for Henry, coming out as an Asian undocumented person provided him with the ability to make visible the issue of Asian immigrant narratives among a largely Latinx movement. In the process, this work ignited within him a desire to build community with fellow Asian undocumented organizers as a means of developing an agenda. While these efforts sparked a conversation, they also placed a great deal of responsibility on his shoulders as one of the only Asian undocumented activists who had publicly disclosed his immigration status with the media and members of the broader community.

In our discussions about his experience coming out as an Asian undocumented immigrant, Henry reflected on how this process also allowed him to recall the initial reasons that his family immigrated to the United States:

I came to the US from South Korea at the age of 11 with my mom and older sister. It was June 25, 2001. I guess back in South Korea one of the main reasons that we came [to the United States] was because of financial difficulties. Our family own[ed] a Japanese restaurant business, but it didn't work out and we eventually had to file for bankruptcy. We were trying to figure out how to continue living in South Korea and a lot of people, not only our family, were facing similar issues because of the IMF's [International Monetary Fund's] impact on the South Korean economy; it was a mess.[14]

The Asian economic crisis of the late 1990s that Henry mentioned provided an important reminder that Asian undocumented immigrants, like their Latinx peers, also faced financial hardship that resulted in their migration. In discussions of undocumented immigration from Latin America, much emphasis has been placed on the role of US-Mexico relations, specifically the North American Free Trade Agreement (NAFTA), and importantly so.[15] Discussions of Asian undocumented immigrants' migration experiences, however, focus primarily on their racial/ethnic identity, often considered a novelty among undocumented immigrant activist spaces, and attention is not necessarily paid to examining the contexts and factors that lead to such migration. However, as Henry's remarks demonstrate, the circumstances that led to his family's decision to migrate to the United States parallel those of many Latinx undocumented immigrants. In a working paper published by the National Bureau of Economics Research, Steven Radelet and Jeffrey Sachs expand upon the connections between the 1990s economic crisis and its effects in Latin America and Asia. Their remarks help put into perspective and illuminate the causes that Henry shared in his personal narrative:

One ironic similarity between the Mexican (1995) and Korean (1997) financial crises is that both countries joined OECD [the Organisation for Economic Co-operation and Development] on the eve of their respective financial catastrophes. There is a hint of explanation in this bizarre fact. Both countries collapsed after a long period of market euphoria. In the case of Mexico, a high-quality technocratic team led the country through stabilization, privatization, liberalization, and even free trade with the United States. Indeed the supposed cornerstone of Mexico's coming boon was admission to NAFTA, which occurred in November 1993, just

ASIAN AND UNDOCUMENTED | 57

months before the collapse. In Korea, a generation-long success story of industrial policy and export-led growth had culminated in Korea's admission to the exclusive club of advanced economies. Korea had even succeeded in democratization without jeopardy to its enviable growth record. In both countries, collapse came not because of a prolonged darkening economic horizon, but because of a euphoric flow of capital that could not be sustained.[16]

This comparison that Radelet and Sachs make regarding the growth of the Mexican and South Korean financial markets underscores the similar nature of the economic and financial situations that contemporary Mexican and South Korean undocumented immigrants faced and that informed their families' decisions to migrate to the United States. Similar to the narratives of Asian undocumented immigration to the United States in the 1800s, the contemporary context of such migration has also become obfuscated by majoritarian scripts and narratives. However, as Henry's disclosure of his own immigration status and his subsequent elaboration of the context that led his family to immigrate makes clear, these community knowledge–sharing practices taking place through storytelling practices, reveal a great deal of nuance within these activists' lived experiences that must be taken into consideration in examining their organizing efforts. The narratives concerning activists' family experiences and migration experiences uncovered through the storytelling process, such as the additional context related to Henry's family, add to the nuancing of the narrative of Asian immigrant experiences that he and other movement activists have undertaken.

Moreover, though other Asian undocumented activists I interviewed, like Henry, were greeted with enthusiasm and invited to take part in coalition-building events across Asian and Latinx undocumented immigrant experiences, not all Asian undocumented organizers' coming-out experiences were similarly received. Anna, an undocumented Filipina organizer from the greater Chicago region, recounted how, when she came out to her peers, she faced questions regarding her legitimacy as an Asian undocumented individual and disbelief that she, as an Asian American individual, could be undocumented. She shared what transpired when she chose to disclose her immigration status in college:

I was always very active in the Asian American and Filipino American communities on campus and many people knew me for being outspoken about issues like educational equity and access and need for greater support for students of color. In my junior year, when I decided to come out [as undocumented] to my friends in these social justice orgs, many—who I had already shared this [with] on a one-on-one basis—did not believe that I could be undocumented. Even those friends I had who were a part of [the campus undocumented student organization] questioned me claiming undocumented status as I had migrated to another country before coming to the US that allowed me to enter with [provisional] status and because I had grown up in a middle-class neighborhood in the suburbs of Chicago.

Although Anna was a longtime participant in Asian American and Filipino American spaces on her college campus, when she disclosed her undocumented immigrant status to her peers, she was met with disbelief and uncertainty. As a member of the Asian American community, a community often associated with the model minority myth, Anna was automatically assumed by her peers to be a US citizen. According to the model minority myth, Asian and Asian American individuals are used to illustrate social mobility and economic success in comparison to other immigrant communities and, increasingly, to white nonimmigrant communities.[17]

As Anna's experiences demonstrate, the notion of a fellow organizer being both Asian and undocumented was unfathomable to her peers. Thus, even while the model minority myth may allow certain Asian undocumented organizers to "pass" as US citizens or legal permanent residents, Anna's example points to her intent to disrupt that narrative and, in doing so, raise awareness regarding the existence of and needs of Asian undocumented communities within broader immigrant rights organizing spaces. Anna's interest in working to advance coalition-building efforts between Asian and Latinx undocumented immigrant communities was stymied by her peers' disbelief. This scenario echoes a phenomenon that sociologist Caitlin Patler has described as the result national origin–based framing of immigration status for many non-Latinx undocumented immigrant communities. Elaborating on this phenomenon and its relationship to cross-racial/cross-ethnic coalition building Patler writes, "Though opportunities for interracial immigrant rights organizing do exist, due to structural racism (in the form of residential and occupation segregation), the possibilities for group mobilization and solidarity are often bound within ethnic communities, potentially posing challenges for interracial coalition building."[18] Anna's own national origin and the broader racial/ethnic community's disbelief regarding her immigration status during her coming-out process led to a missed opportunity for Anna to facilitate coalition-building efforts among Asian and Latinx undocumented communities. Yet, as the narratives later in this book highlight, in her activism Anna, like Henry, consciously worked to overcome this barrier, underscoring the shared experiences across members of both groups. It is therefore not solely residential and occupational segregation that would lead to the differential racialization of Latinx and non-Latinx undocumented immigrants, but for undocumented immigrant youth, the different educational spaces they occupy in the college and university context.

As an illustration of community knowledge–sharing practices, the information that Anna shared with her college peers was critical to facilitating their understandings of not only her family's immigration narrative but also those of the broader Asian undocumented immigrant community. By sharing her family's migration narrative and illuminating the historical context of Asian immigrant communities in the United States and globally as part of her own narrative as an undocumented immigrant, Anna was able to simultaneously assuage her peers' concerns and educate them on the topic. The overall complexity of Anna's own family migration story, however, was not lost on her. During adolescence she and her family moved to a Pacific Island nation whose citizens were also granted US national status. Yet, US national status did not confer US citizenship status and/or legal permanent residency, and thus Anna was still undocumented. This personal experience caused Anna to draw upon discussions of the historical context of US empire building in her explanation of her family members' immigration situation and legal statuses. Anna's incorporation of this historical context is related to the silenced history of Asian immigrants as the first undocumented immigrant community in the United States. The legacy of US imperialism evidenced through the United States' participation in the ongoing colonization of its current territorial possessions and the displacement of indigenous peoples, is a history that many US citizens, and even some activists, are not fully aware of. It is also a history that does not necessarily comport with the model minority myth and contemporary depictions of Asian Americans as consisting solely of "high-skilled," economically mobile East Asian individuals that have come to dominate the racial scripts available to members of this community. By educating herself on this historical narrative and sharing it with her peers through storytelling, Anna became increasingly vocal about her own narrative and positionality as an Asian undocumented immigrant and, in doing so, sought to nuance the narrative—both historical and contemporary— for her fellow movement participants.

As the contrast between Henry's and Anna's experiences and related reception demonstrate, coming out and disclosing one's status as an Asian undocumented individual often functioned as a double-edged sword. Storytelling for Asian undocumented organizers like Henry and Anna utilized a social movement repertoire adapted from LGBTQ activist strategies and tactics: coming out. Coming out as both Asian and undocumented had key implications for the development of these activists' self-awareness and political consciousness and prompted a conversation within the movement that had previously not taken place to such an extent. Asian undocumented activists' use of storytelling was a central technique to engage in community knowledge–sharing practices.

Storytelling and Narrative Sharing: Externally Focused

While storytelling practices largely served as a means of educating others within the immigrant rights movement regarding Asian undocumented immigrant experiences, these efforts were also utilized externally to reshape the framing of undocumented immigration in the mainstream political imaginary. Externally focused events, such as the one described later in this chapter, highlighted for audience members the diversity of Asian undocumented immigrant experiences, even while organizers advocated for the inclusion of a unified Asian undocumented identity within the media, which largely limited its coverage to the case of Latinx undocumented individuals.

Located in New York City, the nonprofit Asian American Writers' Workshop (AAWW) has its offices centrally located in Manhattan, a short subway ride away from Chinatown and the city's Asian immigrant community. In the summer of 2016, the collective hosted an event devoted specifically to discussing the experiences of Asian undocumented immigrants, showcasing a recent graphic novel by Tings Chak.[19] The novel, titled *Undocumented: The Architecture of Migrant Detention*, and the discussion at the event focused on "the intersection of prison abolition and migrant justice . . . [through] counter-narratives that highlight resistance by incarcerated women and migrants."[20] The event itself was co-sponsored by members of two undocumented Asian immigrant–led organizations in New York City: Revolutionizing Asian American Immigrant Stories on the East Coast (RAISE) and Desis Rising Up and Moving (DRUM), showcasing the experiences of local undocumented immigrant activists alongside an expansive overview of the inextricably linked immigrant detention and prison industrial complexes.[21] This connection between Asian undocumented immigrant experiences and the detention and incarceration of immigrant communities worked to align discussions of Asian undocumented immigrant narratives with discussions taking place in the broader immigrant rights organizing community.

At the event, a diverse cross section of community members (students, parents, artists, and activists), both Asian and non-Asian identified, and from high school through retirement age, gathered on a warm summer evening in the AAWW offices. The attendees listened to a transnational narrative of immigrant detention in Canada and the United States. An Asian immigrant architect, Tings Chak, opened the conversation sharing how she conducted interviews with government authorities and community members to provide visual renderings of these detention facilities. This was followed by a question-and-answer session facilitated by Tings Chak. Authors of *Amplify(HER): Raising the Counter-Narrative*, a zine showcasing the stories of undocumented women from the Asian diaspora, were seated at the back of the room selling their zine.

This event's organization—first educating audience members about the unjust practices of immigrant detention, followed by opportunities for discussion with members of the Asian undocumented immigrant community—helped make the issue real and personal to individuals who, though they may have been supportive of Asian American issues, may not have ever met any Asian undocumented immigrants, let alone heard their stories. After the formal presentation, attendees were encouraged to connect with representatives of RAISE and DRUM, some of whom were also authors of *Amplify(HER)*, and learn more about immigrant detention and daily surveillance directly from those who have experienced their effects.[22] Attendees were also urged to sign up and continue learning more about these issues and, potentially, to become involved as supporters of the immigrant rights community. By encouraging attendees to reach out and follow up with the organizations that planned and hosted the event, activists' externally focused efforts helped raise awareness of potential movement participants regarding the multiracial aspect of the undocumented immigrant experience in the United States today.

The zine sold at the event, *Amplify(Her): Raising the Counter-Narrative*, showcased the narratives of Asian undocumented women. It centered these women's voices, mediated through art and creative writing, and provided a much-needed platform for them to share their work with a broader audience. The publication also offered an engaging, interactive medium through which community members could readily learn more about the issue directly from other community members and activists. One of the zine entries, the illustrated story "A Cause Worth Fighting For," by an individual using the pseudonym "One Eyelash," presents an image of the Asian undocumented narrator split down the middle.[23] On the left side are items representing the individual's high levels of academic achievement: a straight-A report card, an honor roll certificate, and a student-of-the-month ribbon. In contrast, on the right side are speech bubbles containing derogatory words and phrases often used to demean undocumented immigrants: "illegal," "get out of my country," and "criminal." These two narratives—high-achieving student and criminalized undocumented immigrant—illustrate the tension faced by undocumented immigrants, including Asian undocumented women whose experiences are showcased in the zine.

The main character in One Eyelash's story reaches a breaking point during high school and the college application process. Multiple barriers emerge as she works on her college application—having to indicate her citizenship status on the SAT application, not being eligible for a summer internship reserved for US citizen and legal permanent resident students, and not qualifying for in-state tuition in a state where she has resided for the past fifteen years. The character then finds that she is identified as "American" on an International Baccalaureate certificate. This reminder reaffirms her hope in the potential for educational success to lead to increased opportunities in the United States despite the xenophobic criminalizing rhetoric that is so pervasive in mainstream media, as depicted at the beginning of the story.

A shared experience among undocumented immigrants, in particular undocumented youth, this Asian undocumented woman's narrative underscores the similarities between Asian undocumented immigrants and their non-Asian counterparts whose access to a K-12 education is protected by the Supreme Court's ruling in *Plyler v. Doe*. Like the experiences of many of their non-Asian counterparts, the story of this Asian undocumented woman includes a moment in which, upon graduation from high school, she finds herself limited by the restricted options she faces as an undocumented student seeking to continue her education. Her narrative underscores the similarities between Asian undocumented and other undocumented students' experiences along the educational pipeline. Much like sociologist Roberto Gonzales's discussion regarding undocumented youth's journey coming to terms with their undocumented status, Asian undocumented youth, like their non-Asian counterparts, face similar challenges and barriers to their pursuit of higher education.[24] Nevertheless, this narrative, while seeking to emphasize the commonalities between these two groups—Asian and Latinx undocumented youth—simultaneously reifies an image of all undocumented youth as high-achieving and college-bound, or what Walter Nicholls has explained as the "DREAMer" identity, tied to the proposed DREAM Act.[25] Scholars have also noted the ways undocumented immigrant youth have pointed to the limitations of a unified DREAMer identity and its effects in promoting narratives that conform to mainstream political discourse.[26] Nevertheless, as the zine example underscores, activists have still found the use of such a framework helpful in forging a common identity among various subgroups within the contemporary immigrant rights movement.

Externally focused and conveyed through a two-part narrative-sharing format—a public presentation and the distribution of a collaborative zine publication—Asian undocumented activists such as those organizing and hosting this AAWW event also focused their efforts on raising awareness of the plight of Asian undocumented individuals among members of a broader public: allies and potential supporters of the undocumented immigrant community. Underscoring the parallel trajectories of Asian and non-Asian undocumented individuals in the US K-12 education system and the connections between the prison industrial complex and the treatment of Asian, Latinx, and black undocumented immigrants, the event highlighted the importance of solidarity and coalition building as a primary goal. At the same time, this event drew heavily on the narratives of self-identified Asian undocumented women and Asian immigrant women allies to make its case and promote an ongoing conversation among those in attendance. Consequently, the zine presented at the AAWW event also provided a space for resistance, one that welcomed the participation of fellow community members through an engagement with a social justice–oriented public.

The Strategic Leveraging of an Intersectional Movement Identity

Building on community knowledge–sharing practices, Asian undocumented organizers' participation in immigrant rights organizing spaces focused on bringing further awareness to the importance of employing a multiracial approach in the movement. Such efforts, while seeking to create space—both physical and socioemotional—for undocumented activists from different racial/ethnic identities, involved a careful balance of emphasizing the necessity of constructing a unifying narrative while not losing sight of the importance of recognizing differences among participants' identities. As enacted by Asian undocumented organizers, the Identity Mobilization Model's second strategy, the strategic leveraging of an intersectional movement identity, took two primary forms. These forms consisted of (1) voicing the concerns of Asian undocumented community members in predominantly Latinx immigrant rights organizing spaces and (2) creating Asian undocumented organizing spaces for participants to develop their own agenda prior to engaging in coalition-building efforts. While the Asian undocumented activists I interviewed for this book discussed the importance of working to increase the visibility of their experiences and others like them in broader immigrant rights organizing spaces, they also discussed the necessity of having specific organizing spaces to build community and develop a set of priorities related to their unique intersectional identities as Asian and undocumented individuals. This dual-pronged approach, of simultaneously utilizing their Asian undocumented identity both to discuss issues of undocumented status within the broader Asian immigrant community and to build coalitions with their non-Asian undocumented activist counterparts, demonstrates the multiple frameworks and causes that activists must balance due to the intersectional identities they hold. As the discussion regarding coming out or disclosing one's immigration status as an Asian undocumented individual illustrated, these organizers' strategic use of an intersectional movement identity has led to activists' emphasis on coalition building, but also to their simultaneous recognition of the needs of the multiple communities to which they belong. In this case, they must also balance this desire to build coalitions and raise awareness of Asian undocumented communities as part of the broader immigrant rights movement with the need to increase awareness regarding the role of legal status in shaping the lives of Asian immigrant community members.

Shared Asian and Latinx Undocumented Immigrant Organizing Spaces

Many of the activists I spoke with shared how coming out as an Asian undocumented individual served an important, empowering role in understanding their sense of self and in facilitating their engagement in social movement activism. These individuals also detailed how their embrace of their newfound identity influenced their participation in social movement spaces that were led predominantly by Latinx-identified individuals. Drawing on their own intersectional Asian undocumented immigrant identities, these activists voiced their concerns in these predominantly Latinx undocumented immigrant spaces working to reinforce broader movement efforts to focus on the cultivation of stronger ties between Asian and Latinx undocumented activist communities and to publicly present a broader, multiracial front. In these narratives, what becomes clear is the desire to embrace a heterogeneous movement identity while also acknowledging and affirming difference among the identities that movement activists hold.

For example, consider the following. At a large public university in the San Francisco Bay Area, Azucena, an undocumented Latinx student, organized a community conversation at the campus multicultural student center to discuss the limitations of an overarching DREAMer identity.[27] Explaining her reasons for holding this event, the first in a series of community-wide conversations, Azucena discussed the tension between the creation of an overarching movement identity such as a DREAMer identity and the internal divisions it reproduced among movement participants. She shared:

> For me I definitely found a transition between the DREAMer identity being discussed in a positive way in 2009 [when] there was a positive discussion around that identity [and] later on as new legislation came about [such as] new forms of aid for undocumented students and then [the] influence of radical undocumented groups organizing [which brought about] a lot of negative stuff around [the DREAMer identity]. . . . [Members of those radical groups] were like DREAMers are stupid [and] they aren't helping us [movement participants to advance our cause] . . . [so] I tried to create spaces where we could invite members of the community who were saying these things to have a dialogue around it.

Azucena's original interest in providing a space to discuss the implications of the DREAMer identity focused primarily on internal debate and critique of its use among members of the undocumented immigrant community. Yet, as the following account of the event demonstrates, considering the limitations of an overarching DREAMer identity also helped open space for discussions of other identities that movement participants held, in particular their racial and ethnic identities.

At this community gathering, undocumented college students shared their frustrations with the term "DREAMers"—namely, how it is imposed on them and has shifted attention away from the undocumented immigrant community as a whole, including their parents and other adults. "I really dislike the word 'DREAMer,'" Alejandra said. "For me, it doesn't capture my experience. Yeah I'm in college and pursuing a degree at a top university, but I had many struggles getting here [to this university]. I'm not perfect, and I am not just a high achiever as the term makes me out to be." Voicing her critique of the DREAMer label, Alejandra's comments demonstrated the limitations of the term and its impact on individual students whose overall identities include much more than solely their student status. Another student, Adriana, added, "This reminds me of the concept of market citizenship we discussed in a [sociology] class I am taking. Basically, undocumented students are being characterized as worthy of citizenship based on their ability to work and contribute to this country." As Adriana's comment pointed out, undocumented students and community members not only were aware of the limited scope of DREAMer identity but also were able to quickly and effectively articulate their critique by drawing upon personal and academic justifications.

[handwritten margin note: market citizenship]

Continuing this critique of labels imposed on undocumented immigrant communities, Susan, an Asian undocumented student, shifted the conversation from an interrogation of the term "DREAMer" and provided another layer of analysis. She remarked, "I want to add that I think we need to pay attention to the numbers of students like me who are Asian and undocumented on campus. I've heard administrators say they know that more than half of the undocumented students on campus are Asian Pacific Islander. But we don't ever talk about what that means and how we can best serve these students. I'd like to see that change." Susan made use of an opening in the discussion, where attendees pushed back against framings of deservingness and respectability, and filled it with the narrative of Asian undocumented students on campus to call for greater resources and services for this student community. She did so in a forum that brought together Asian and Latinx undocumented students to reflect on their needs as part of an internal campus community conversation. In doing so, Susan drew upon the finding that, unlike the national undocumented immigrant population, in which 76 percent of individuals come from Latin America, on their campus Asian undocumented students made up almost half of the undocumented student body. She stressed that these students had few formal resources as compared with their Latinx counterparts.

Rather than use this moment in the conversation as a divisive one, Susan used this shift productively. In the discussion and the dialogue that ensued, Susan and her peers made connections between the historical narratives of Asian and Latinx undocumented immigration and the contemporary everyday realities of the undocumented students attending their university. These connections worked to counteract misconceptions regarding Asian undocumented immigrant experiences and, in the process, built solidarity and emphasized similarity with their Latinx undocumented peers. Also, when Susan brought the conversation regarding the problematic nature of the DREAMer identity back to the context of her campus and its unique racial dynamics, the discussion that ensued underscored how the limitations of a DREAMer framing of undocumented youth's identity can in fact open up a broad range of other related conversations such as the assumed racial identity of DREAMers.

Asian Undocumented Specific Organizing Spaces

Acknowledging the critical need for Asian undocumented activist participation in predominantly Latinx undocumented organizing spaces, Asian undocumented community members also discussed the importance of having the space and freedom to develop their own agenda prior to considering how it might (or might not) relate to that of their Latinx peers. Through the formation of Asian undocumented activist spaces, members of this community have engaged in community-building efforts that have led to the politicization of a collective Asian undocumented immigrant community. Functioning as a space for activists to explore the intersectional nature of their Asian and undocumented immigrant identities, these groups subsequently served as a springboard for Asian undocumented activists to cultivate coalitions between their own movement organizations and predominantly Latinx immigrant rights groups.

I first became acquainted with members of this San Francisco Bay Area Asian undocumented student–led organization through my role as a graduate student research assistant for a university-based research project that sought to examine undocumented students' experiences in social movement activism.[28] According to the organization's mission statement on its website, its members saw their work as rooted in emphasizing their personal experiences as Asian undocumented individuals and in sharing these experiences through the use of personal narrative. The members also viewed the goal of bringing attention to the silenced narratives of Asian undocumented migration as dovetailing with creating community spaces, devoted solely to the needs of this community. The group's focus on supporting Asian undocumented students from across the San Francisco Bay Area was related to the research project's efforts to assist UC Berkeley in increasing Asian undocumented students' participation in the campus-wide conversation around improving resources for all undocumented immigrant students.

Following up from the initial meeting I held with members of the organization, I interviewed Kamol, an Asian undocumented student from the San Francisco Bay Area and one of the group's members, regarding his participation in the organization and in the broader immigrant rights movement.[29] Kamol shared:

> So [organization name] is a support group but it's also where I grew in my activism. I don't think I am really a full activist at all, but in terms of the DREAM Act that's where I learned [how to get involved in activism]. I started doing phone banking and writing to all these senators in their offices. I attended rallies and went to the [state] capitol a lot to speak with lobbyists. Through this process I refined my story and received training on how to organize and how to put pressure on the media to cover issues important to my community.[30]

As Kamol's response illustrates, even though he may not have initially seen himself as an "activist," through participation in the organization's efforts to build community with fellow Asian undocumented youth, he was able to learn ways to become involved politically, should he decide to do so. Attending rallies and speaking with lobbyists, Kamol learned many of the strategies such as storytelling and narrative sharing encompassed within the community knowledge–sharing processes and how to use these strategies to achieve a political goal. This training gradually led Kamol not only to become more comfortable taking part in political activism but also to begin to see himself, like Henry, mentioned earlier, as an example for his peers: "I [now] want other Asian undocumented students to see that there are others like them involved in the movement and I think that, by showing by example that's one of the way[s] you can really have students come out [and speak about their experiences as undocumented people]. [I feel this way] because it sucked going through high school for me not knowing anyone [else who was undocumented] and it was really tough at times. But now it's different."

For Kamol and other Asian undocumented activists with whom I spoke, community specific spaces like the organization discussed here had important benefits for Asian undocumented youth and also facilitated subsequent community-building efforts between Asian and Latinx undocumented students from different campus- and community-based organizations. While Asian undocumented activists repeatedly emphasized the importance of cross-racial/cross-ethnic organizing spaces, it was equally important for them to have their own spaces in which to dialogue and explore the multiethnic nature of Asian immigrant identity in itself.

A few weeks after interviewing Kamol, I was invited to an event where members of this organization and of the campus's predominantly Latinx undocumented student group held a joint potluck at the school's Latinx-themed house. This potluck was an important opportunity for Asian and Latinx undocumented community members to reach outside their respective community spaces and get to know one another. The Latinx-themed house provided subsidized housing to undocumented students and became a recognized welcoming space for students on campus. Based on the event's description, one of its goals was to explore the potential for the theme house to do the same for Asian undocumented students. The event began with a dinner consisting of dishes brought by the attendees and representing traditional foods of their various cultural heritages, from the Philippines, South Korea, China, Japan, Mexico, and El Salvador. After the meal, we transitioned to introductions, with each individual sharing briefly about the food they brought and its significance for their family or community. Azucena, one of the student leaders at the Latinx theme house, gave us a tour and introduced us to residents who were spending time with one another during this end-of-semester Sunday evening.

Following the meal and tour, everyone gathered in the living room to play games and eat dessert. This was an intimate space that included members of both groups. As we wrapped up the gathering, Tricia, one of the Asian undocumented individuals in attendance, asked, "Can we do more events like these? I've never been to [the Latinx theme house] before. It's a really nice space!" Hoa, another Asian undocumented attendee, followed up, "Do you guys have openings for next semester? I'd want to live here. It's affordable and so close to campus." "We do have openings," Azucena replied. "And it would be great to have you come and join the house. We have an application process, but I can send you the information and walk you through the process."

This informal gathering of Asian and Latinx undocumented students at the university's Latinx-theme house demonstrated the importance of organizational spaces, both group-specific and multiracial gatherings for movement participants. More specifically, while organizations for specific racial or ethnic identities served an important role of facilitating community building and equipping members for engagement in political activism, they also functioned as a conduit for preparing members to take part in the cultivation of meaningful coalition-building efforts with other movement participants. By strategically leveraging their identities as Asian undocumented individuals, the organizers interviewed for this book illustrated the purposeful and necessary use of identity as a means of propelling a movement forward. As part of this process, these organizers extrapolated from their personal lived experiences through their participation in organization spaces and used their identities— both individual and collective—to contest the limitations of the US racial hierarchy that seeks to treat racial/ethnic groups differentially and in an isolated manner. Within the US racial hierarchy, Asian and Latinx undocumented immigrants are, in Laura Pulido's term, "differentially racialized."[31] The differential racialization of Asian and Latinx immigrants has its roots in the period of post-1965 Asian immigration rather than the exclusion and criminalization of Asian immigrants from the late 1880s to early 1940s in the United States and the Western Hemisphere more broadly. Yet, through the forging of intimate personal ties across racial/ethnic lines, these activists have worked to transcend the limited and often oppositional framing of Asian and Latinx immigrant communities wherein Latinx individuals are viewed as the prime example of undocumented immigrants and Asians are viewed as members of the so-called model minority.[32]

High-Stakes Allyship: Personal Experience and Family Background as a Key Motivating Factor for Social Movement Participation

"The primary participants in th[is] action will be directly affected individuals," Pilar, an undocumented organizer from Chicago, informed those in attendance at a meeting of undocumented activists and allies. The political action that Pilar was referring to was an act of civil disobedience protesting the federal government's increased deportations of undocumented community members. "We are focusing on the narratives of undocumented community members because our stories are often the ones that are not told and are instead told by others," Pilar added referring to mainstream media depictions of undocumented youth, or DREAMers, as solely seeking to assimilate into mainstream US culture through excelling in academics, not social movement activism.

During this meeting, other movement allies and I listened to the undocumented activists and sought to assist in furthering the group's goals as best we could. As allies we were assigned many of the tasks that could potentially put undocumented organizers in jeopardy in terms of their ability to participate in the civil disobedience action. Here I use the term "allies" to refer to US citizen and legal permanent resident supporters of the contemporary immigrant rights movement. Often these tasks included interaction with police officers or other government officials who, in the process of working with undocumented organizers, may inquire about an individual's immigration status and in turn detain an organizer or set of organizers, preventing an action from being carried out. Allies participated in a manner that allowed them to come alongside directly affected individuals and movement leaders. As a result, their efforts did not detract from undocumented organizers' ability to carry out a given action in which an emphasis on the risk to which undocumented activists subjected themselves (often, the risk of deportation) was a key aspect of the action itself. Movement allies' efforts instead assisted directly affected participants in engaging in "high-risk activism" that would produce the visual and rhetorical spectacle that the given action was working to produce.

As an ally for this particular civil disobedience action, I was assigned the role of "caretaker" for the only Asian undocumented activist in the group. I had come to know this activist through my participation in the social movement organization, and we had become good friends. Through our shared racial and ethnic identities as Asian individuals, and because of my background as the son of a Southeast Asian refugee mother, we developed a connection and sense of trust that facilitated our ability to work together.

For this action, caretakers were responsible for, as the name indicates, taking care of an individual participant's needs: being present and helping during the action itself, communicating with family members in case a participant was held in jail overnight, and reassuring the participant during the course of the event that a dependable and reliable support network was available to them. The activist for whom I served as a caretaker had not disclosed to her parents that she was participating in the action. In the event that the activists were to be held overnight, I would coordinate with her sister, who would then relay the news to the family, potentially after she had been released. I took this responsibility to carefully communicate such sensitive information to this individual's family very seriously. Having this responsibility also underscored for me that there are varying degrees of allyship, especially in a movement context. In this case, depending on how the local police officers responded to our action, allies or caretakers also might have been in jeopardy of being arrested.

In this action, my participation as a caretaker was a form of emotional labor, which ultimately supported activists' goal of centering the voices and lived experiences of directly affected individuals. Through this support, however, I did not seek to take away from the fact that these directly affected movement participants were placing a great deal on the line. If they were arrested or detained, and if Immigration and Customs Enforcement agents were called, they could find themselves removed from the country for exercising their political voice. This was a very real danger that directly affected movement participants faced but that allies, even high-stakes allies, did not.

The individuals who participated in this action were physically connected to one another during the action through makeshift devices created to make it more difficult for them to be arrested and therefore were unable to move their hands, resulting in their needing assistance in drinking water, eating, and wiping away tears that some of them shed while waiting to be arrested by local police officers. While sitting in a circle blocking the gate through which vehicles leaving the detention center exited, the Asian undocumented organizer whom I was assigned to care for was crying when the police arrived and asked me to come over to wipe her tears. At this point the police had not yet begun to arrest the participants and were still allowing other organizers and movement supporters to approach those about to be arrested. I gradually approached the circle of organizers seated in front of the detention center gate, pulled out a small package of tissues, and wiped this organizer's tears from her cheek. Just then, a media photographer took a picture of us, making use of this moment of anguish for the organizer for whom I was caring. Though I sought to support this action from afar, my role as a high-stakes ally placed me in the center of this moment, being included in the photograph and subsequently asked to answer a series of questions following the news reporter's brief interview with this activist. The inclusion of high-stakes allies in carrying out this action and the media's documentation of the event that included allies alongside movement participants underscore the ways that directly affected movement participants and high-stakes allies often collaborated to carry out key movement actions.

Through this experience serving as a caretaker for this particular Asian undocumented activist, I began to consider more critically not only my own participation in this action but also the broader role of allies in the contemporary immigrant rights movement. Reflecting on this issue, I remembered how my own familial connection to the issue of Asian immigration was a key motivating factor in my participation in this action and the movement more generally. Given my mother's experience as a Southeast Asian refugee whose family fled to the United States due to US military intervention in her home country, I felt a strong personal connection to the issue of Asian immigration. From my elders I had learned how, as refugees, my mother's family was afforded a fast-tracked process to gaining citizenship, while others who arrived under different circumstances were not given the same treatment. I therefore saw the experiences of all Asian migrants and immigrants more broadly as interconnected and tied to a shared fate.

Allyship, in this case high-stakes allyship, was activated by my connections to the movement organizer taking part in the action—an Asian undocumented activist—and my own familial ties to the issue. These connections are built from both community knowledge–sharing practices in spaces that include both directly affected movement participants and allies, leading to the creation of a new category of allies, what I have termed "high-stakes allies." In the case of movements in which participants' rights and presence are unrecognized under the law, high-stakes allies demonstrate the importance of looking at the complex network of individuals whose lives are also affected when undocumented communities are threatened. The activation of this network of allies who, through the dual connections of their own participation in movement spaces and their familial background, are able to come alongside and support the critical work of Asian undocumented activists underscores the critical impact such efforts can have, while still working not to eclipse the foundational work that directly affected movement participants have undertaken.

Conclusion

Teasing out the specific processes through which Asian undocumented activists have utilized the Identity Mobilization Model's three interrelated strategies in their social movement participation, this chapter has highlighted the effectiveness of an intersectional identity in cultivating coalitions with members of similarly situated groups. Given the highly racialized nature in which undocumented immigration is discussed in the United States today, Asian undocumented activists have worked most closely in forging ties with the Latinx undocumented community.[33] This process begins with Asian undocumented activists becoming more familiar with their own community's immigrant histories, a process that has been elevated through community knowledge–sharing processes, and putting this heightened awareness into action with the strategic participation and involvement of Asian undocumented organizers in Asian and Latinx immigrant organizing spaces. These coalitions are important in broadening the base of participants involved in the immigrant rights movement, but they also provide an important space for activists to reflect upon their movement's overarching goals and purpose. This work also entails discussions focused on incorporating both Asian citizen and legal permanent residents and Latinx undocumented immigrants, using the unique positionality of Asian undocumented immigrant community members as a bridge to doing so.

3

Undocuqueer Activism

The Use of Shared Tactics across Social Movement Contexts

Undocuqueer activists' leadership in the immigrant rights movement has led to an overlap in the use of strategies across the LGBTQ rights and immigrant rights movements. In an interview with *Latina* magazine, Tania Unzueta, an undocuqueer organizer from Chicago, described the importance of the National Coming Out of the Shadows (NCOS) event in the scope of undocumented immigrant activism. In the process, she elaborated on the event's role in raising the broader public's awareness of the immigrant rights movement's adaptation of LGBTQ activist strategies: "Our [the Immigrant Youth Justice League's] first Coming Out of the Shadows Day, which ended up turning into a month-long observance, took place in Chicago in 2010. 'Coming out' is a tactic stemming from the gay liberation movement. It allowed people to use their own stories to fight against stereotypes. This is powerful. And we [undocumented immigrant organizers] found that when we said we were undocumented, even in our own private spaces, it was also empowering to us as individuals. It connected us, created community and allowed us to organize in ways we hadn't before."[1]

As Tania's remarks point out, LGBTQ activist strategies such as publicly "coming out" or disclosing one's identity as queer have been subsequently adopted by other movement activists, including the immigrant rights movement.[2] Yet, immigrant rights organizers' adoption and subsequent use of queer activist strategies were not a mere coincidence. Rather, the reappropriation of queer activist strategies has been led by self-identified undocuqueer activists who have drawn upon the strategy to emphasize the multilayered "coming-out" processes that these community members undergo in disclosing their queer and undocumented statuses. This chapter demonstrates the role undocuqueer leadership has played in the immigrant rights movement (similar to the experiences of

Chapter focus

Asian undocumented activists) and how this has, in turn, influenced the borrowing of strategies across movement contexts.

Drawing on the theoretical framework of repertoires of contention, defined by sociologist Donatella Della Porta as strategies that are "handed down [across] generation[s] of activists," I argue that "coming out" can and should be read as a cross-movement repertoire given its adaptation from queer activist struggles to the context of undocumented immigrant political activism.[3] This argument dovetails with the discussion of how coming out, as in the case of Henry and Anna, facilitated the incorporation of Asian undocumented immigrant narratives in the movement, highlighting the use of the strategy across movement subgroups but in a different context: undocuqueer activism. In making this argument, I build on the work of sociologist Veronica Terriquez, who found that the use of queer activist frames in the context of the immigrant rights movement has resulted in a case of social movement spillover, which was magnified by the boomerang effect: the bidirectional influence of each movement on the other.[4] Building on this finding, I argue that activists have gone beyond borrowing and adapting strategies from other movement contexts and, instead, have utilized these processes to forge coalitions between queer and undocumented immigrant movement groups. Thus, by embracing their multiple marginalized identities, undocuqueer organizers active in both the immigrant rights and LGBT movements have undertaken key bridge-building work to develop a collective undocuqueer identity as part of the undocumented immigrant movement.[5]

Utilizing the Identity Mobilization Model framework, this chapter explains the shift from adaptation of another movement's strategic and tactical repertoire to the cultivation of an intersectional political consciousness. The chapter begins with an overview of how undocuqueer organizers have utilized the coming-out strategy to raise awareness both internally and externally regarding the importance of an intersectional framework that takes into account both sexual orientation and immigration status. This discussion is followed by an examination of undocuqueer activists' participation in queer and immigrant rights organizing spaces and their role in voicing the concerns of being both queer and undocumented. The chapter concludes with an analysis of how undocuqueer activism, while noteworthy in its bringing together of two contemporary social movement spaces, can be read as contributing to the development of an expansive reading of immigrant rights activism that encompasses Asian undocumented and formerly undocumented communities.

The Identity Mobilization Model in Practice

Undocuqueer activist experiences highlight the theoretical and lived realities of being both undocumented and queer and the subsequent marginalization that occurs from inhabiting these identity categories. As undocumented people, undocuqueer activists face the daily threat of deportation. As queer individuals, members of this community are also directly impacted by the nation-state's investment in maintaining and (re)producing heterosexual norms and values.[6] Through the lens of the Identity Mobilization Model, it becomes clear that these activists have not let their social positioning dictate their ability to engage in radical, transformative social change. Instead, as part of the fight to secure increased rights for all undocumented people, undocuqueer activists have strategically navigated the contours of their undocumented and queer identities, connecting the individual with the structural as part of sustained engagement towards in increasing opportunities for all immigrant community members.

Complex Storytelling Practices: Laying the Groundwork for Emerging Conversations

For undocuqueer organizers, similar to their Asian undocumented immigrant counterparts, community knowledge–sharing practices have functioned as an important resource to convey information both within the movement and externally to a broader public. More specifically, these internal and external processes have paralleled those enacted by Asian undocumented immigrant activists, with internally focused efforts working to raise the awareness of immigrant rights organizers regarding the importance of foregrounding queer immigrant experiences within the overall movement. Externally focused events such as the National Coming Out of the Shadows rally that Tania mentioned at the beginning of the chapter have been geared primarily toward raising the visibility of undocumented immigrant narratives, including undocuqueer narratives, in terms of how the immigrant rights movement is viewed within the mainstream public imaginary. Combined, these internally and externally focused effects have underscored the importance of an intersectional movement identity as embodied within the experiences of undocuqueer organizers and its impact on the social movement mobilization of undocuqueer activists alongside their Asian undocumented and formerly undocumented peers. Additionally, while largely informal in nature, community knowledge–sharing practices have also worked to highlight activists' ability to cultivate an oppositional consciousness, or shared understanding and critique of an overarching social issue.

Storytelling and Narrative Sharing: Internally Focused

Self-identified undocuqueer activists' efforts to raise awareness regarding queer issues within the immigrant rights community were often rooted in the personal yet used mechanisms other than personal narratives to educate their peers on the issue. The disclosure of one's personal narrative facilitated through the coming-out process, described in the previous chapter in connection with Asian undocumented organizers' efforts, had a highly transformative effect as organizers sought to build community and gain visibility within the movement. Yet, undocuqueer organizers have used film and media to promote such conversations within the undocumented immigrant community and personal narrative sharing externally to gain the support of potential movement allies.

One such instance in which film was used to promote an internally focused movement conversation was a screening at the University of Illinois at Chicago. On a cold, windy Chicago weekend afternoon in March 2013, I met a group of immigrant rights organizers on the South Side, where we connected with María, one of the group's lead organizers, who then drove us a few miles away to the university campus. After arriving and finding a parking space, we began the trek to the building where the screening would take place. Though the campus was fairly empty given that it was the weekend and classes were not in session, we had parked in a visitor's lot that was quite a distance from the building where the screening would take place. I was excited about this because it meant that I would get to see more of the campus, a university that many of the activists with whom I worked had attended.

Members of the organization who had attended the university as undergraduates took the rest of us on a short tour of the campus before we arrived at the location where the film screening would take place. While passing the student center, the campus's main hub, we encountered an interesting sight: a series of massive posters, the size of the front of the buildings we were passing, hanging from the windows with the faces of some of the group's members. Initially unsure of what to make of the posters, I asked Diana, a graduate of the university and one of the group's main organizers, about them. She told me that the posters were part of a university-wide campaign to raise awareness about the experiences and needs of undocumented students at the university. The university had commissioned these large posters, showcasing images of the students' faces and including quotes about participants' experiences as undocumented students on campus, to demonstrate that there were in fact undocumented students at the university and to show that the campus was a welcoming space for them. Holding the event at a university with such a public, open commitment to supporting undocumented students made a great deal of sense. This was a space where many of the group's organizers had attended college, felt comfortable, and had preexisting connections with faculty and staff. This was also a space that these organizers thought would be welcoming to undocumented community members who were not students or who were considering matriculating at a college or university.

After walking through campus for fifteen minutes, we finally arrived at the building where the screening would take place. It appeared to be the annex to a larger classroom building and was equipped to fit approximately twenty-five to thirty participants. Immediately after we arrived, we set up the snacks and ordered pizza as we waited for some of the other event organizers to arrive. As attendees gradually trickled in, it seemed that the audience would be on the smaller side due to the cold, windy weather and the fact that many students, one of the event's primary audiences, were likely to be busy working on homework or other school-related tasks before the start of the coming week.

After a brief introduction, the first film, *Milk*, was loaded onto the computer and screened. The film chronicled the life of gay politician

Harvey Milk, who was assassinated in 1978 and who is remembered as one of the most vocal openly gay activists in California at the time. For two and a half hours it captivated many of the audience members, given its difficult content and the homophobia portrayed in the film that was directed at Milk and his peers. After the film ended, everyone in the audience took a brief pause before transitioning to the collective discussion regarding its message about the importance of supporting and acknowledging LGBTQ social movement activism. The screening was meant to provide an educational space for audience members to watch a set of films and engage in a collective discussion of the relationship between queer and immigrant rights struggles. Interestingly, while many of the event's organizers had already seen the film, they expressed their excitement about watching it again and engaging in a discussion with their peers and fellow community members afterward about its significance, especially in the context of the immigrant rights movement.

Having been involved with this organization for almost six months at the time, I assumed that the discussion would be highly spirited, especially given the film's focus on such an iconic LGBTQ rights activist. Moreover, as someone who had taken courses on social movement studies and read about the social and historical contexts of different social movements, I imagined that the discussion would center on the fact that many of the film's characters were white gay men and how an expanded perspective of queer identity was being taken up in the immigrant rights movement through a focus on queer immigrants of color.[7] Instead, surprisingly, there was an uncertain and anxious feeling in the room, with folks seeming to still be processing Milk's death, which occurs in one of the final scenes, and the fact that, even in the United States, he was assassinated for his outspoken activist nature, fighting for a cause that directly impacted him.

The screening provided a space for movement participants to reflect on their own identities—primarily undocumented and queer—and the relationship of these identities to their continued activism and participation in the immigrant rights movement. Yet, this silence underscored for me the gravity of the situation that undocuqueer individuals faced: deportation by the government due to their immigration status compounded by the potential to be the target of hate crimes as queer individuals. Given that many of the attendees were key leaders in the contemporary immigrant rights movement, I could feel the sense of gravity that this had for these undocuqueer activists. Thus, the silence among those in attendance seemed to point to a broader issue—the emotional toll that activism has taken on individuals, especially those inhabiting multiply marginalized social positions, what sociologist Deborah Gould has referred to as an affective approach to examining emotions in a social movement context. According to Gould, an affective reading "carv[es] out a conceptual space within the emotional turn for the noncognitive, nonconscious, nonlinguistic, and nonrational aspects of the general phenomenon of emotion."[8] Sitting with one another, in community, and processing the film together was an experience that did not necessarily require dialogue or an actual articulation of what individuals were experiencing. Rather, it was the participants' nonverbal, affective emotional response to what they had just seen that was particularly telling in this moment. Elaborating on how this process takes place, Gould explains, "I use the term *affect* to indicate nonconscious and unnamed, but nevertheless registered, experiences of bodily energy and intensity that arise in response to stimuli on the body. These experiences are *registered* in that the organism senses the impingent and the bodily effects, but *nonconscious* in that this sense making is outside of the individual's conscious awareness and is of intensities that are inchoate and as yet in articulable."[9] This unconscious but ever-present bodily response and emotional engagement with the material also served as a healing experience for the individuals in the audience because processing the material in this manner provided a means for participants to process, collectively, the risks they were taking in their work—the risk of detention and deportation but also the risk of being harmed because of their sexual orientation—and the meaning of these risks for their own lives and the overarching goals of the movement.

Given the general tiredness and the heavy emotional toll that *Milk* had on those in the audience, the event's organizers decided to still screen the next film, *Sleep Dealer*, but to skip the discussion following it. A futuristic science fiction film dealing with issues of border security, surveillance, and border economies, *Sleep Dealer* held special meaning for some of the organizers who had met the director—Alex Rivera— during a visit he made to Chicago a few years earlier. Juxtaposed with *Milk*, *Sleep Dealer* dealt with difficult issues that were frequently discussed in immigrant rights organizing spaces: the mistreatment of immigrant community members, the hyperpolicing of undocumented border crossers, and the underground economy that had developed to provide access to resources among marginalized community members. The film was familiar to many in the audience and underscored the injustice of the contemporary immigration system, portraying what it might become if left unchecked. This film seemed to leave those in attendance a bit more upbeat given that it clearly pointed to the target of the activism in which they were engaged: an increasingly criminalizing and oppressive immigration system.

After the second film ended, the attendees event were visibly tired—physically, given the number of hours we had sat in the room watching the films, and emotionally, from discussing and processing very "heavy" and difficult topics. Taking this into account, some of the organizers mentioned that perhaps in the future showing and discussing one film might work better and increase turnout. Everyone was encouraged to take some pizza home, and some students headed directly to the campus library to finish up homework in preparation for the upcoming week.

Along with some of the event's primary organizers, I caught a ride back to the South Side, where a group of us ate dinner at a Mexican restaurant in a predominantly Latinx immigrant neighborhood. Over dinner, we engaged in community building meant to affirm group members' positionality as undocumented and predominantly undocuqueer activists seeking to engage in important movement activism, but also to support one another in their navigation of everyday life. As already mentioned, the films did a highly effective job of illustrating the very real challenges that undocumented immigrants, queer individuals, and undocuqueer community members face on a daily basis. As we took some time to reflect on the event and to check in with one another, the dinner space functioned as a means of offering an upside to often taxing and difficult discussions around the multiple marginalizations that movement activists face. Through community knowledge–sharing practices, which took place as part of the film screening and brief discussion, this group of undocuqueer organizers in Chicago actively worked to increase the visibility of undocuqueer identity as part of the broader immigrant rights narrative. These activists' efforts were successful in alerting their peers to the very real effects that being undocumented and queer has on movement participants' ability to thrive as individuals and as social movement organizers. Yet, the dinner after the event made clear the transformative effects that recognizing difference and the implications of difference can have on building community and leading to the empowerment of movement participants, in particular those identifying as both undocumented and queer.

Storytelling and Narrative Sharing: Externally Focused

Externally focused, with the goal of reaching a broad segment of potential allies and promoting a broader approach to undocumented immigrant identity, one that is empowering and affirms intramovement difference, National Coming Out of the Shadows rallies are another critical space in which storytelling and narrative-sharing practices have occurred. A form of community knowledge–sharing practices, the externally deployed narratives shared at NCOS rallies have built on the internal conversations that activists have had regarding best approaches for incorporating queerness into the movement's overarching focus on the plight of the undocumented immigrant community. Activists have then reframed these internally focused conversations in a manner that can be shared publicly and appeal to movement supporters and allies. In the process, immigrant rights organizers have successfully engaged a broader community—both their own and a greater public—around the importance of the intersection of undocumented and queer identities. This is illustrated both through the leadership of undocuqueer activists in creating the NCOS event and through their participation in the event, sharing their own narratives and experiences with those in attendance.

Begun in 2010 in Chicago as a one-day event with the intent of affirming the humanity and lived experiences of undocumented community members, NCOS soon grew into a national movement. As part of the event's growth and its eventual spread across the nation, members of the organization that first planned and staged the event soon developed ways to adapt and hold an NCOS event "in your community" and "at your school," pointing to the ways that the event's originators viewed it as something to be taken up and adapted by others.[10] While the previous chapter mentioned how Asian undocumented activists used NCOS events to raise awareness of their community's experiences among a broader public and to encourage other Asian undocumented youth to take part in political activism, this discussion of NCOS focuses on its origins and, in particular, the use of the coming-out metaphor to describe both queer and undocumented immigrant experiences.

Having recently moved to Chicago, where I was attending meetings of a local immigrants' rights organization, I soon noticed a reoccurring agenda item: NCOS. Unsure of what NCOS stood for, I leaned over and asked one of the other meeting attendees sitting next to me if she could fill me in and provide some context for the discussion. "National Coming Out of the Shadows," she quickly explained. I later learned that NCOS referred both to the yearly undocumented youth-led rally held in Daly Plaza in downtown Chicago and to the monthlong set of events across various locations. NCOS's performative aspect, wherein individuals went onstage to openly disclose their undocumented identities and share what is was like for them to lead undocumented lives, was extremely powerful and moving for me to observe as an ally. In 2013, the year in which I attended my first NCOS event, the focus was on "those being criminalized by the federal government and immigration enforcement: people in deportation proceedings, people in detention, those who do not qualify for deferred action, and those with past interactions with the law."[11] This investment in contextualizing and exploring the narratives of individuals at the margins of an already marginalized identity demonstrated the importance of these community knowledge–sharing practices in broadening the scope of the identity category of undocumented immigrant individual.

In a YouTube video, Cindy, a Chicago-based organizer explained, "By coming out to share our stories we put a face to the issue [of undocumented immigration]. We are human." In this publicly posted video, Tania, another Chicago-based immigrant rights organizer, shared, "We are not here asking for acceptance. We are asking for change. Coming out means telling a friend, a loved one, a classmate, a teacher, something that we would have otherwise kept private. It is using our lives and our stories as a political tool for change."[12] Reinforcing both Cindy's and Tania's points, another Chicago-based organizer, David, stated, "March 10th [National Coming Out of the Shadows Day] . . . is sharing our stories and publicly coming out as undocumented to kinda step away from that fear that for most of us as children we are instilled to not share your status [as] you might be tak[en] away."[13]

Taking a narrative- and storytelling-based approach, these events also included important educational content regarding the experiences of undocumented immigrants in the United States, providing an opportunity for intergenerational dissemination among youth organizers in the cities where the events were held. For undocuqueer activists in particular, NCOS events held a unique significance, as this public "coming-out" experience varied depending on whether activists had already come out as queer individuals or whether, in their immigrant "coming-out" narrative, they also chose to include a discussion of their queer identity.

The 2013 NCOS rally I attended in Daly Plaza in downtown Chicago did not have a specific focus on an undocuqueer identity but had a wider emphasis on "coming out" as movement strategy and the importance of sharing one's story as an undocumented immigrant whose very presence in the United States is criminalized. As part of these narratives, speakers recounted the heavy surveillance they were subjected to by the police and federal immigration agents and the fear that this surveillance instilled in community members. As Rose Cuison Villazor has noted, these tactics have cast undocumented immigrants into the shadows, similar to how regulation of sexuality has forced queer-identified individuals "into the closet." Consequently, the surveillance of undocuqueer community members is multifaceted and manifests in a variety of ways.

Working to break the constraints of both the shadows and the closet, some self-identified undocuqueer activists participated in various iterations of NCOS in the city in which it began: Chicago. Speaking about her experience sharing her story during another NCOS convening, Luna, a formerly undocuqueer individual from Chicago, remarked: "[So] I didn't help organize [the event] but [I] actually shared my story at the second Coming Out of the Shadows [event] that the Immigrant Youth Justice League organized. It was a really great [experience] because I had gone to the first [NCOS event] and I . . . felt very inspired. To me it was a call to action, you know? And participating in the second one was definitely amazing." Coming out in this very public way as an undocumented individual was, as Luna explained, an empowering experience and one that she chose to take part in largely due to what she saw and experienced during the first NCOS event. The public and performative nature of this form of narrative sharing and storytelling underscores the ways these individual acts of undocumented organizers' social movement participation had far-reaching effects in terms of inciting others to do the same and, in doing so, to reflect on their own reasons and goals for participating in the immigrant rights movement. Looking back on the experience, though, Luna added, "I don't think I was out as queer [when I came out as undocumented at NCOS]." Coming out as undocumented prior to coming out publicly as a queer individual points to the importance of examining the relational and also layered experiences of identity for social movement activists. Thus, while Luna was drawing upon a technique and strategy that had been developed by queer activists, she had not yet disclosed her sexual orientation to her family member or her peers. The relationship between the two movements and the coming-out strategy, however, was an aspect of the action that Luna felt very strongly about emphasizing in her response. She shared: "You know it's important to mention that this idea of coming out comes from the gay liberation [movement] that was [tied to their experiences] coming out of the closet. [Something I often think about is] what it meant then and what it means now for us [as undocumented people] to come out as a way to show that we're kind of everywhere and we're all sorts of people." Clearly seeing the connections and parallels between the strategies employed in the immigrant rights and queer liberation movements, Luna disclosed her undocumented status first and did so in a very public, visible manner at NCOS. Later, when coming out as queer, Luna grappled with what it meant to be both undocumented and queer, or undocuqueer. At this point, though, she had already taken an active role as an engaged leader in the immigrant rights movement, perhaps facilitated by her having already come out as an undocumented individual.

While Luna's public disclosure of her undocumented status empowered her to embrace her identity as an undocumented individual, it also elicited mixed reactions from her family members. Discussing their reactions, she added:

[Participating in NCOS] definitely brought up interesting discussions with my family because . . . it brought up to them that I was gonna be doing this thing and at the time although my mom was involved [in the movement] I think that she still had a lot of fear, like [fear about] our family being superpublic about our status . . . and of what could happen.

Like, will people at their jobs find out? I remember she [asked me to] not mention their names and things like that.

As these comments demonstrate, the empowerment that Luna felt as a result of her participation in the NCOS convening also underscored for her the broader sense of fear that undocumented individuals face on a daily basis. Though her mother, as Luna explained earlier in our interview, had first become involved in the immigrant rights movement through a local church and introduced Luna to these organizing spaces, there was still the question of positionality in terms of how undocumented youth and other family members saw their vulnerability as undocumented individuals. For Luna, her identity as an undocumented young person, someone who had grown up in the United States and received her K-12 education and was in the process of completing her college degree, positioned her in a unique way to make rights claims upon the US nation-state. As sociologists Shannon Gleeson and Roberto Gonzales argue, undocumented youth's experiences in the US education system and their early age of arrival have led to their socialization in a manner that has facilitated their ability to make such rights claims.[14] The role of Luna's mother in introducing her to these movement spaces in the first place, however, points to the ways in which political socialization in this context can occur in a bidirectional manner and indicates that the boundary between undocumented youth and worker might be more porous than it initially seemed. Explaining her mother's critical role in her political involvement, Luna told me:

So I became involved in immigrant rights organizations in approximately 2008 or 2009 and I was still in high school at the time. My mom was [pretty familiar with the local church organizing group] and it was a really rough time [for me] because the counselors at my school were telling me that I wasn't going to be able to go to college because of my [immigration] status. . . . And I remember even being kind of bratty, like, "Oh my god, Mom, let's get out of here" . . . but eventually through attending I met the founder who [was] undocumented herself and had gone to [college name] and graduated. And the moment I met her and that I heard she had gone to school and graduated . . . I [decided to become] more involved.

As Luna's experience points out, externally focused instances of narrative sharing and storytelling are rich sites for examining how activists' individual identities lead to their participation in social movement activism, as well as the various interconnected issues that they invoke. In Luna's case, though she later identified as an undocuqueer movement organizer, during the time of her participation in the NCOS event, she had not yet come out as queer. Also, the reaction by her family members, particularly her mother, to her participation in the event points to the importance of examining the positionality that undocumented youth hold relative to other members of the undocumented immigrant community and how this positioning has allowed them to be uniquely situated in order to take part in this work. For undocuqueer and other movement participants who hold intersectional identities, their participation in the movement and their engagement with the movement's broader efforts to empower all immigrant community members are shaped primarily by their identities as undocumented individuals, but also by other intersecting identities they hold, such as also identifying as queer. The public act of sharing their stories with a broader public can be read not only as a manifestation of this intersectional consciousness, but rather as providing a glimpse into the unfolding of a complex process of identity formation, one that, as Luna's narrative demonstrates, impacts political mobilization and the potential for coalition building with members of other similarly situated groups, but which is also related to a variety of other factors and circumstances.

The Strategic Leveraging of an Undocuqueer Intersectional Movement Identity

Undocuqueer activists' participation in queer and immigrant rights organizing spaces, similar to the participation of their Asian undocumented counterparts in predominantly Latinx spaces, can be understood as constituting a diverse set of experiences and approaches. Yet, as a whole, these experiences can be seen as working to forge an enduring dialogue between undocumented and queer communities in a manner that affirms the intersectional nature of these individuals' identities and assists them in the alliance-building process. These efforts have had a three-part effect, highlighting (1) the challenge of inserting the narratives of migrants and people of color into predominantly white, nonimmigrant, and middle-class queer organizing spaces; (2) the importance of including sensitive discussions of queer issues in intergenerational immigrant rights organizing spaces; and (3) the creation of a specifically undocuqueer-focused activist space. Because the exchanges that have occurred in these spaces have proved both fruitful and challenging, as this section demonstrates, these discussions have ultimately prompted much-needed conversations that, in turn, have led to openings for dialogue between organizers in LGBTQ and immigrant rights movement spaces. As I argue, this work and the creation of space for an emerging conversation, has been integral to the cultivation of and utilization of an intersectional connection in both movements.

Undocumented Activists' Participation in LGBTQ Organizing Spaces

Undocuqueer-identified activists' participation in LGBTQ organizing spaces was often relayed by interviewees as a difficult and challenging experience. These LGBTQ spaces that activists referenced, located in large cities across the country, were largely mainstream organizational spaces that focused on achieving marriage equality.[15] While not necessarily reflective of all LGBTQ organizing spaces nationally, the following instance, described to me by James, an undocuqueer organizer residing in Chicago, points to the decisions that activists had to make in navigating their participation in mainstream LGBTQ movement organizations. James's story begins with an abrupt conversation in which he was informed that he would be fired from his job due to his immigration status. Recounting the conversation in which he was called into his boss's office, James explained: "I was working for a business using my college degree when one day my boss called me into her office. She was changing hiring companies, and they were updating information in their computers. She told me that my social security number came up as not matching. I froze and then proceeded to tell her about my undocumented status and how I did not have a Social [Security number]. She had to let me go because she could not pay me. . . . [T]hat was a really horrible experience." As his account makes clear, James lost his job due to his immigration status as an undocumented person residing in the United States. Though he had completed a rigorous undergraduate degree in a specialized field requiring technical training and expertise, graduating from one of the top universities in the area, it was ultimately his immigration status that prevented him from being able to be employed in the field, not the other hurdles that often deter or prevent students from pursuing this career. Yet, after losing his job, rather than seek out immigrant rights organizing spaces, James was drawn to an LGBTQ organizing space. As a result, he attended Human Rights Campaign meeting on Chicago's North Side.[16] This was an experience that, as he explained, did not allow for full expression of both his undocumented identity and his queer identity:

> [Because of this experience being let go from my job,] I then started to get involved in local nonprofit organizations, attending a few of the Human Rights Campaign meetings. . . . When I went, I noticed all the people there were white, middle class, and the meeting was held in the North Side, really far away from where my family lived, so I stopped attending. When I would bring up immigrant rights issues, they would always ask how it was related to marriage equality and the LGBT community. Later, when I was active in [immigrant rights organization], I met the director of the Chicago branch of the Human Rights Campaign at [a social justice community event] and told her about my experience with their organization. She apologized for me being treated that way and said they had been working to make the space more inclusive for folks from diverse backgrounds, but that there was still a lot of work that needed to be done.

The challenges of participating in an LGBTQ organizing space that did not take an intersectional approach to sexuality caused James to feel that he needed to hide and ignore a critical aspect of his identity: his undocumented status. This was particularly curious given that he had been fired from his job was due to his undocumented status and this was one of the primary motivating reasons he sought to participate in activist spaces in the first place.

Seeking to introduce a discussion of immigrant experiences into queer-focused spaces, James also described how he repeatedly found his efforts rebuffed by fellow members of the organizing space. This led him to seek out more inclusive spaces that brought together discussions of queer and immigrant identities, which he ultimately found as part of his involvement in undocumented immigrant organizing spaces. Joining an undocumented youth–led organization, James eventually immersed himself in the immigrant rights organizing community, becoming one of the organization's two cochairs, and he works to welcome other undocumented young people into the space and organizing more generally.

Also, while James did not find an inclusive experience in the Human Rights Campaign meetings, this is not to say that no LGBTQ organizing spaces are inclusive of these other identities. This organizing and the work they were doing happened to be the most visible to individuals, like James, who were looking to become involved. Though his initial involvement in LGBTQ-oriented activist spaces was challenging, as an undocuqueer-identified individual, James was later able to bring a critical focus on queer identity into his work in immigrant rights organizing spaces. Drawing on his own positionality as an undocuqueer individual, James took part in broader efforts to incorporate discussion of undocumented immigrant status within mainstream LGBTQ movement spaces and vice versa. As a result, he found a welcoming community of other undocuqueer-identified individuals in immigrant rights movement organizing spaces, spaces in which he was able to fully embrace his queer and undocumented identities and be mentored by fellow undocuqueer organizers.

At the conclusion of our interview, James explained how he later ran into some of the Human Rights Campaign organizers he had met during the first few meetings he attended on the North Side. Having become one of the key leaders in the local immigrant rights community, he explained to the Human Rights Campaign activists why a critical focus on queer identity, but also its intersection with immigration status and other identities such as one's racial/ethnic identity, is important. These organizers apologized to him and pledged to reach out in the future, perhaps to collaborate on the planning of some upcoming events and rallies. As James's narrative highlights, the inclusion of undocuqueer issues, in particular the intersection of immigration status with a queer identity, is largely the result of undocuqueer activists' participation in and navigation of these multiple movement spaces. Undocuqueer activist's efforts to increase the visibility of these issues in mainstream and radical queer organizing spaces point to the dual role that undocuqueer individuals' participation in these spaces has had on both the immigrant rights movement and the LGBTQ rights movement.

Discussions of Queer Identity in Immigrant Rights Organizing Spaces

While the immigrant rights movement's undocuqueer leadership has helped create a welcoming space for LGBTQ conversations, some difficult conversations have also occurred in these spaces given the deep roots of faith-based organizations in the immigrant rights movement.[17] In fact, the Catholic Church has played a significant role in the success of the immigrant rights movement in the late twentieth century. As a result, some undocuqueer organizers with whom I spoke described the complex decision-making processes they underwent in deciding when and how to disclose their queer identities to their fellow undocumented immigrant organizers. Doing so led to the strategic use of an undocuqueer identity in immigrant rights movement spaces.

Recounting his experience during a summer 2012 campaign to raise awareness regarding immigrant rights in light of the upcoming presidential election, Felipe, an undocumented activist from the San Francisco Bay Area, shared his excitement at being able to work with individuals from different geographic locations and age-groups. In our discussion, however, he also explained the differences he saw regarding the individuals with whom he was comfortable sharing his identity as an openly queer undocumented person:

> So . . . you know . . . there was also a tension around queerness and undocumented status between some of the older folk and younger folk, for example, I remember one of the young folk saying, you know, I'm not going to pretend like I'm not, I'm not going to show that I'm not queer because it's against [your] religion. You know, the thing was that some of the people taking in a lot of these folks in the [campaign] were religious organizations and like churches, and some of them were pro-immigrant rights but were homophobic. And so that created some tension for some of the intergenerational [conversations].

As Felipe's comments suggest, the variation within organizers' public presentations of their identity to fellow activists and the broader public has been complicated by the differences in undocumented youth's and adults' general perspectives on queerness, a tension that exists within the larger immigrant rights community. Felipe's narrative points to the challenge of reconciling the religious identities of many of the older movement participants with the large contingent of undocuqueer leaders among younger generations. Additionally, even within the undocuqueer community, important variations exist among activists in their approaches to their queer and undocumented immigrant identities: individuals may choose to foreground one over the other or to embrace the two simultaneously. While these decisions varied for each individual, the majority of activists interviewed asserted that such decisions should not be judged or compared. Instead, each interviewee acknowledged the difficulty in strategically choosing which identity to assert in a given situation, despite the immigrant rights movement's broader reputation for being a largely inclusive space for queer community members.

Undocuqueer individuals' efforts, in both LGBTQ and undocumented immigrant organizing spaces, have been crucial to pushing the boundaries of inclusivity in each movement. Taking an active role in leadership positions in both immigrant and queer rights organizational spaces, undocuqueer activists have worked to increase the visibility of queer issues within immigrant rights organizing spaces and, in doing so, have attempted to make such spaces, even intergenerational ones, more inclusive.[18] This contingent of outspoken undocuqueer leaders in both movements has also helped shape the development of a more expansive and inclusive "immigrant rights agenda," one that welcomes discussion of intersecting and related social identities and experiences of marginalization.

Undocuqueer-Specific Organizing Spaces

As James's and Felipe's experiences, discussed earlier, demonstrated, some immigrant rights or LGBTQ rights organizations were not inclusive of an intersectional framework in their approaches to organizing. Yet, as explained by David, the undocuqueer activist from San Francisco whose story opened this book, this led to the need to create their own spaces in which undocuqueer individuals could attend to the specific needs of their community. Theorizing the importance of undocuqueer as a subject position and the importance of undocuqueer-specific organizing spaces, David stated:

> Eventually I became involved in organizing spaces [catering] directly to issues facing queer and undocumented youth or, as we call ourselves, undocuqueers. For me this was a very fruitful experience as I was able to connect, network, and build solidarity with other undocuqueers. It also allowed me to help bring discussion of gender and sexuality in conversation with those around the topic of undocumented students and the DREAM Act. Many times people forget the pervasiveness of sexuality present in immigration laws and policies and how while some undocumented people might be able to fix their status through marriage, [we] undocuqueers do not have that option.

For David, having a space to combine his queer and undocumented identities, and to focus solely on their intersections, was important for the development of a robust and transparent discussion of the meaning of identifying as an undocuqueer individual. Yet, though this gathering worked to bring together undocuqueer individuals from across the country, it highlighted the diversity even within the community regarding lived experience, politicization, and whether individuals had disclosed their queer and/or immigrant identities to their families and community members. Describing the importance of reaffirming the heterogeneity within the gathering, David commented:

> And another interesting thing that played a big factor [about us coming together at the first national undocuqueer convening] was that within community, within *familia* [family], and within ourselves some of us are out to each other, but you know some of the folks [in the space] weren't out to their families yet or weren't out to other communities, other undocumented communities within their respective hometown or where they were living in. And that was also very interesting because you kind of saw the type of silencing that happened in multiple levels in terms of not only community organizing and activism, but much more specifically

within the home and people who are closely related to you. And so for most of us I think it was eye-opening see that we were all in very different places.

Noting the range of ways that undocuqueer individuals have embraced and explored their own intersectional identities both publicly and privately, David's comments bring to light the importance of acknowledging the heterogeneity within the various subgroups of the movement. This heterogeneity is reflected not only within the multiple identities of undocumented immigrant subjects but also within the subgroup of undocuqueer individuals.

While the creation of specific organizations for undocuqueer-identified individuals served an important purpose—facilitating community building and the cultivation of a group consciousness—there were instances of immigrant rights organizations that did work more proactively to include the experiences of undocuqueer community members, owing in part to the growing role of undocuqueer leadership in the immigrant rights movement. Luna, a formerly undocumented and queer organizer from Chicago, explained:

> Being involved in [immigrant rights organizations] and at the time being queer and undocumented . . . all of those identities that I held were recognized and the work that I was doing felt like it encompassed all of those things, you know what I mean? Because there were times I tried to get involved in the gay organization in college or other places or organizations that just dealt with immigration, but it was very difficult to find a good space in those organizations as they were fully recognizing one part of me, but not the other. Finding a space, especially on like [immigrant rights organization name], it felt like, you know, I could bring my whole self to that space and the work I was doing.

The Chicago-based organization that Luna took part in and joined during her years in college, as she indicates, served as a welcoming space that supported individuals who identified as undocumented but also held other key social identities such as being queer. For undocuqueer organizers, the creation of an undocuqueer-specific space, or those that took seriously the nexus of these two experiences, facilitated these internal group conversations. In the process, this allowed for these individuals to, through their leadership in immigrant rights and LGBTQ rights organizations, shift the discussion in these spaces regarding inclusion of related but often overlooked aspects of movement participants' lived experiences.

High-Stakes Allyship: The Incorporation of Individuals with Close Personal Ties to Directly Affected Movement Participants

The Identity Mobilization Model's third strategy, high-stakes allyship, refers to nondirectly affected individuals' participation in movement organizing spaces. Recall that these individuals may maintain a close relationship with or be related to individuals who identify as being directly affected by an issue but hold certain rights and privileges that allow them to come alongside directly affected individuals as allies. The term "directly affected individuals" emerged in the movement organizing spaces in which I participated, and in the context of the immigrant rights movement, referred to undocumented individuals.

A welcoming setting for undocumented activists to openly share their experiences as undocumented people, "shout-it-outs" in Chicago provided an empowering and uplifting space for activists to build community alongside one another. According to Camila, an undocumented activist based in the greater Chicago region, shout-it-outs can be understood as "something that we [organization members] would do once a month. . . . We would invite people in the [undocumented immigrant] community . . . [and] we would promote it as a safe space, meaning that no reporters were there and very few allies were present. It was mostly undocumented [people] speaking to [other] undocumented [people] in the beginning, and it was more of the beginning stages of people feeling comfortable [sharing] their stor[ies]." As a setting where self-identified undocumented individuals gathered and were free to share their emotions and frustrations as undocumented persons residing in the United States, this space was unique. Yet, as Camila mentions, it was not exclusively limited to self-identified undocumented individuals. Rather, the allies who were allowed to participate were carefully chosen and, as she elaborated later in the interview, often had a personal connection to the issue. Although they were similar to the storytelling and narrative-sharing practices detailed as part of the community knowledge sharing–practices strategy of the Identity Mobilization Model, these stories shared in the shout-it-out setting illustrative of high-stakes allyship differed in that they were undertaken in a closed space, meant for a mixed but carefully chosen audience, and illustrated a moment when the lines between directly affected individual and movement ally were shown to be increasingly complex.

While there were few allies present, shout-it-outs also, on occasion, provided the space for allies to become politicized. As the case of James, an undocuqueer organizer from Chicago, illustrates, the space served as a means of both building community and incorporating new members into a broadened formulation of how the undocumented immigrant community was constituted. During our interview, James shared his experience inviting and accompanying his partner to a shout-it-out event. Yet, as James explained, at first his partner was interested in learning more about shout-it-outs for a class assignment that he needed to complete: "I remember when I first went [to the shout-it-out]. . . . I went with my boyfriend because he wanted to write a paper for school and he wanted to get to know the people that were part of [organization name], an organization that is very much on top of the line of the immigration movement. He wanted to get to know them in a personal way, like really get to know these organizers and what they have in their backgrounds and what's encouraging behind them." Unbeknownst to his partner, James too was undocumented. While James did not initially plan to use their joint attendance at the event as an opportunity to disclose his status to his partner, surrounded by a community of other undocumented, largely undocuqueer, community members, he decided to do so. He continued:

> I went there without him knowing that I was undocumented. I just
> thought that I would go there so that he wouldn't feel completely weird.
> So I went [to the event] and these people are sharing their stories, which
> I remember [activist name] was there and [activist name] and [activist
> name] were too. I started to feel like I could relate to [the activists who
> were sharing their stories] and so I decided [unexpectedly] to come out
> as undocumented to my boyfriend even though I didn't plan to. It was a
> very emotional time for me and it's still very emotional because at the end

of the day, [being undocumented] is not just a term that is given to us, but it's also a [form of] oppression that really affects all the relationships we have with other folks.

For James, the shout-it-out event provided a highly supportive space that he could attend when he wanted to be in community with other self-identified undocumented individuals. Though not all attendees identified as activists, the event's organizers were also leaders in a Chicago-based undocumented youth–led organization.

When he accompanied his boyfriend to a shout-it-out event, primarily to help his partner complete a school assignment around an issue that he was interested in learning more about, James felt moved and took the opportunity to share his own undocumented status with his partner. In doing so, James was able to embrace fully the multiple aspects of his identity that, combined, facilitated his involvement in the immigrant rights movement, and he invited his partner to support him in the process as a high-stakes ally. Through a close, intimate understanding of the issue as shared by his romantic partner, James's partner could, in turn, become politicized and engage in a form of allyship that, while acknowledging his nondirectly affected participant identity, also underscores his close connections to a directly affected person in the movement. High-stakes allyship can thus be understood not only as a category inhabited solely as a result of an individual's relationship to a particular issue but also as a role that developed as a means of supporting directly affected movement activists and furthering the goal of the social movement.

For James's partner and other potential high-stakes allies, their participation in the immigrant rights movement can also be understood as playing a formative role in furthering the movement's overall goal: increased rights for all undocumented individuals. Through the incorporation of high-stakes allies, included in the movement due to their close relationship (familial or romantic) to a directly affected movement participant and the overlapping nature of their own identities (e.g., queer) with movement participants, these individuals represent an important source of support that could have potentially gone untapped. Bringing these individuals into movement organizing spaces, undocuqueer activists like James were strategically and intentionally seeking to provide a more holistic representation of their own identities and to do so in a way that allowed their partners to support them in their social movement activism. At the same time, through this personal connection to the movement, high-stakes allies, like James's partner, not only supported the directly affected individuals to whom they had a close, personal relationship but also often became politicized and active participants in the immigrant rights movement on a broader level. This broader participation in the movement included accompanying the person with whom they held a close personal relationship to movement events (e.g., protests and rallies) and, at times, also choosing to take on leadership roles in their own right.

While examples such as James's partner's politicization as the result of entering movement organizing spaces points to high-stakes allyship's role in terms of bringing those from "outside" the movement "into" more intimate movement spaces, there also were instances in which the internal heterogeneity of movement organizing spaces was reflected in the enactment of high-stakes allyship. At the time of this writing, a migrant caravan, one of a series of caravans, was approaching the United States' southern border, with participants preparing to seek asylum upon arrival.[19] Members of the caravan consisted of a broad range of individuals, including queer individuals, unaccompanied minors, and others seeking refuge from US-precipitated violence. In anticipation of their arrival, the Trump administration coordinated with the Mexican government to enact strict border enforcement at Mexico's own southern border with Guatemala.[20] President Donald Trump also threatened to close the United States' southern border to prevent the caravan's entry into the country. Months earlier, another caravan that included trans immigrant women from Mexico and Central America arrived at the US-Mexico border. Many of these women were placed in detention upon arrival and were kept there until they either won their case or were deported to their country of nationality.

During a warm, humid summer day in New York City, I attended a late-afternoon event that sought to mobilize allies of these detained trans undocumented women from the caravan. The event was focused on having attendees writing letters of support and encouragement to the women to raise their morale and encourage them to continue fighting their cases, if that was what they desired. Of the individuals in attendance, some identified as undocumented activists, many of them leaders in the organization that hosted the event, while others identified as US citizen allies. As I explain later, this letter-writing event was a critical manifestation of the importance and complexity of high-stakes allyship enacted both by other undocumented individuals and by US citizen allies.

A theoretical framework for examining the unique form of allyship that individuals with close personal connections to a social movement enact, this example illustrates the strategy's complex role when considering activism and activist identities in an intersectional context. Expanding the notion of high-stakes allyship to include the participation of US citizen allies with their own personal or familial migration backgrounds alongside the allyship of undocuqueer individuals supporting their fellow trans undocumented activists highlights the term's versatility and explanatory power. Sitting in the same room and engaging in the process of writing letters of support to the trans undocumented women in detention, attendees—both those who identified as undocumented (often undocuqueer individuals) and US citizen allies—engaged in the critical work of centering not only undocuqueer but also trans undocumented women's experiences. Additionally, after learning a bit about the women's personalities and experiences from a caravan participant who was in attendance, attendees were asked to reflect on their own positionality in relation to these trans undocumented women's experiences as they decided what to write in their letters.

My own letters described my experience growing up as the son of a Vietnamese/Cambodian refugee mother and Bolivian immigrant father. As someone who has been involved in immigrant rights organizing in multiple contexts, I wrote letters to the leaders of the caravan, who had been unjustly placed in solitary confinement for their role in galvanizing other caravan participants. I also wrote to those who were described as quieter and who kept to themselves because I sympathized with those individuals as someone who does not like to be at the forefront of an event or campaign but enjoys supporting and assisting those who do.

Ultimately, this letter-writing event brought together undocuqueer and US citizen ally communities to get to know one another and build bridges as they collectively sought to support trans undocumented women in detention. The potential of such an event to bring together two uniquely positioned groups of allies whose interests and experiences converge around a specific subissue within the immigrant rights community highlights the importance of a lens of high-stakes allyship. Moreover, this event can also be understood as laying the groundwork for continued collaboration between the two groups of individuals in attendance (undocuqueer and US citizen allies) and as underscoring the fact that high-stakes allyship is a versatile and dynamic term that encapsulates multiple forms and types of allyship enacted by key stakeholders in the immigrant rights movement today.

Conclusion

Leveraging the strategies laid out in the Identity Mobilization Model, undocuqueer activists have drawn upon their own identities and lived experiences to facilitate coalition-building efforts between undocumented and queer communities. Similar to the plight of their fellow undocumented immigrant community members, undocuqueer activists' efforts have simultaneously focused on the cultivation of a subidentity within a broader undocumented immigrant identity while also affirming the importance of a broader undocumented identity in uniting multiple subgroups within the immigrant rights movement. Inhabiting a unique intersectional identity, undocuqueer activists have purposefully and intentionally drawn upon their own identities and lived experiences to work toward the creation of a more socially just world. Elaborating on this point as part of an interview conducted for an online media series, Mateo, a self-identified undocumented transgender and queer activist shared the following:

> It is hard to decolonize our minds. We have been indoctrinated to believing that there is a duality to everything and that there is a binary system and that anything outside of that is wrong. And so for me, part of my way of framing the world is also to . . . understand . . . that it is not only me breaking through those binary systems, but it's also supporting my community and my family to break those [binaries]. The immigrant justice fight has been really grounded in the same binary that everything is put into. It is the good DREAMer, the bad DREAMer. And so for me I have an issue with the word DREAMer because it leaves out the community members that have the least support from the system, that are already criminalized, that are already being detained, that are already be-

ing put into the school-to-prison pipeline. . . . My activism and my way of organizing is a very holistic approach to fight back against systems of oppression. To me it's really looking [at] and being intentional about intersections because we are such complex individuals. No one here is just an immigrant or just low income or just queer . . . we are a community that is so complex. And for me because my identities are trans and queer and having had my background as undocumented that's the fight that I hold the closest, but it's being mindful of the multiplicity of identities.[21]

Mateo and other self-identified undocuqueer activists' focus on the intersectional nature of undocumented immigrant identity, in this context showcasing the intersection of undocumented and queer identities, points to the ways that activists in the both the immigrant rights and LGBTQ rights movements have been impacted by the organizing of undocuqueer activists in the contemporary period. By placing multiple intersectional undocumented immigrant experiences in conversation, immigrant rights activists have strategically drawn upon openings in the political and legal landscape to foreground the multiple facets of an undocumented immigrant identity. Doing so recognizes the dual importance of movement heterogeneity while also working toward the construction of a broad overarching collective movement identity.

4

Formerly Undocumented Activists

Complicating the Divide between Directly Affected Movement Participant and Ally

As the experiences of the formerly undocumented activists whose experiences are discussed in this chapter demonstrate, the shift from federal classification as an undocumented immigrant to an individual holding formal legal status in the United States is an important yet also extremely challenging transition. After having lived as undocumented immigrants for years, often for decades, these young people now find themselves processing the meaning of their new legal status and their privilege relative to their still undocumented peers. Elaborating on this shift, Juana, a formerly undocumented activist who had previously resided in the San Francisco Bay Area, explained, "[So] I adjusted [my immigration status] last year [and] I had a little bit of a crisis around that, this has been part of me for so long, my immigration status it has been such a huge part of my identity. And with the adjustment of status, that shifted. So people still kind of think of me within . . . undocumented spaces and whatnot, but I mean, it's real, the privilege [of now having status] is real. And I just have to be hyperconscious of folks that I'm working with or talking to. Yeah, [of] having those privileges." For Juana, adjusting her immigration status took place quietly, and others knew about it only if she consciously decided to share about the process, in particular her fellow activists. Activists like Juana recounted how much of this experience was, as in the case of their Asian undocumented peers, isolating. The isolation these formerly undocumented activists described stemmed largely from their uncertainty regarding who to tell and how this might alter their relationship to their undocumented peers. Thus, as Juana's narrative and those of other formerly undocumented activists discussed in this chapter demonstrate, despite this shift in classification by the federal government, the effects of being denied access to legal status in the United States are cumulative and endure even after individuals have adjusted their immigration status.

In this chapter, I argue that the cumulative effects of being an undocumented immigrant during adolescence impact an individuals' sense of self and, relatedly, their approach to engaging in social movement activism. This work can be seen as in conversation with that of sociologists Cecilia Menjívar and Sarah Morando Lakhani regarding the impact that the adjustment of immigration status plays in the lives of undocumented immigrants, especially those who have lived in liminal legal positions for extended periods. They write, "In some cases, study participants' personal and social metamorphoses led to desirable outcomes and, in their view, to lasting improvements in their lives; in other instances, such changes led to less desirable results or to situations that cannot be so easily classified into 'good' or 'bad.' In any case, our emphasis is on how these transformations are substantial, seemingly long lasting, and the result of conscious decisions, which illustrate how viewpoints, mentalities, and the self may be altered in anticipatory and durable ways via the legalization process to have a spillover effect beyond the application itself."[1] Thus, this chapter draws upon the notion of illegality as a continuum, one that shifts over time and is highly contextualized. As the narratives that follow demonstrate, immigration status is not fixed but a fluid and continually shifting identity.

More specifically, this chapter focuses on the experiences of a unique subgroup within the category of formerly undocumented individuals: formerly undocumented immigrant women of color. Interdisciplinary literature on migration has importantly discussed the experiences of immigrant women of color and these women's intersectional lived experiences.[2] By conceptualizing these formerly undocumented individuals' experiences in an intersectional manner—acknowledging these movement participants' experiences as formerly undocumented immigrants, women, and people of color—this chapter works to provide a more holistic approach to examining the continued participation of these community members in the movement as they undergo this key shift in their identity and also their sense of self. Examining the relationship between the multiple intersectional identities that these formerly undocumented immigrant women hold, the narratives in this chapter contribute to literature on the intersection of gender and migration by examining their impact on participation in social movement activism. Utilizing the Identity Mobilization Model, I illustrate how a multifaceted identity, in this case as formerly undocumented immigrant women of color, can be marshaled to cultivate coalitions with other members of the immigrant rights and broader social justice activist community. Through this process, it becomes clear that the gendered nature of migration and migrant illegality is also central to understanding immigrant political activism in the contemporary political moment.

Relevant to this discussion of formerly undocumented women's participation in the immigrant rights movement is the shift that occurred in activist spaces—organizations, rallies, and community meetings—in which I conducted fieldwork for this book toward an intentional centering of the experiences of "directly affected community members." As discussed previously, I understood this phrase as referring to the importance of foregrounding undocumented immigrant community members' voices in discussions of political organizing and strategy. Such a call was often deployed in response to the hypervisibility of the activism by staff members in organizations working on behalf of, rather than necessarily alongside, immigrant communities. While the distinction between allies and directly affected individuals initially seemed clear to me as a self-identified ally and US citizen, I noticed that formerly undocumented individuals, those who were previously considered directly affected individuals, hesitated to consider themselves directly affected after their immigration status had been adjusted. Taking the cue from these discussions regarding the distinction between ally and directly affected individual for formerly undocumented activists, this chapter also works to explore the porous nature of this divide. This approach echoes Justice Brennan's comments in the US Supreme Court case *Plyler v. Doe* regarding the intended temporality of one's undocumented status.[3] As such, it also highlights the ways these individuals navigate the boundary-making and boundary-remaking processes within the movement between these two categories: ally and directly affected individual, something that scholars in the immigrant rights literature have begun to address through an examination of the growing prevalence of mixed-status families in the movement.[4]

As in the prior chapters, I begin with a discussion of the Identity Mobilization Model's utility in explaining the continued participation of formerly undocumented individuals, in particular formerly undoc-umented immigrant women of color, in the contemporary immigrant rights movement. The chapter then provides an explanation of the im-portance of considering the intersection of immigration status, race, and gender for understanding how, through their continued participation in the immigrant rights movement, these activists have constructed and leveraged their individual and collective identities as a tool for orga-nizing. Through this analysis, I explain how formerly undocumented immigrant women of color have leveraged their multiple intersectional identities with regard to the other social identities they hold and how this process relates to cumulative efforts of advancing the immigrant rights movement's agenda. This analysis culminates in an examination of how drawing on their experiences as formerly undocumented immigrant women of color has resulted in stronger ties between these community members and their Asian undocumented and undocuqueer-identified peers.

The Identity Mobilization Model in Action

Focusing on the experiences of formerly undocumented women of color activists, this chapter illustrates the Identity Mobilization Model's utility in examining the socially constructed and shifting nature of legal status as an identity category alongside other social identities, namely, race and gender. As the following sections demonstrate, when movement par-ticipants' legal status shifts, as in the case of formerly undocumented activists, other intersectional identities serve as important pathways along which these individuals negotiate their participation in move-ment organizing spaces. Also, though these activists no longer identify as directly affected individuals, their other marginalized identities over-lap with those of directly affected individuals and, combined with the cumulative and ongoing effects of having been undocumented for such a long period of time, function as a bridge to continued participation in the movement.

Complex Storytelling Practices: Narrative Sharing Enacted through
Emotional Care Work and Mentorship of an Emerging Generation
of Undocumented Immigrant Activists

All the formerly undocumented immigrant women of color I interviewed for this book shared the importance of an intersectional identity
in their conceptualization of their identity and their engagement in
political activism. However, each interviewee described a different
journey in terms of how she navigated her multiple social identities. A
key underlying connection across these women's experiences was their
interest in mentoring future generations of undocumented activists
through community knowledge–sharing practices, which, as discussed
earlier, encompass a diverse set of educational practices in a variety of
social contexts. For these formerly undocumented immigrant women
of color organizers, community knowledge–sharing practices played
out in the form of academic pipeline programs and music education/
artistic expression to support the consciousness-raising efforts among
a younger generation of undocumented immigrant youth. The broad
range of contexts in which these community knowledge–sharing practices occur underscores their central importance not only to how these
formerly undocumented women continue their participation in social
movement organizing but also to the individual nature of each woman's journey as she processes this experience of shifting from a directly
affected movement participant to an ally.

During our follow-up interview, Juana explained how she had moved
to a new city and begun a doctoral degree program, in which she was
studying the activism of undocumented immigrant communities in a
transnational context. Juana also shared how many of the current participants in the contemporary immigrant rights movement belonged to
a younger generation and, as a result, saw her as an "elder" in the community who had fought for rights that many of these younger organizers enjoyed and that facilitated their involvement in social movement
activism in the first place. In describing her newly assumed mentoring
role in the movement, Juana shared how she was often asked to speak
on panels and to continue to be a visible presence in the undocumented
immigrant community despite having adjusted her status. Though she
was no longer directly subject to the threat of deportation as an undocu-

mented immigrant, as a formerly undocumented individual who had lived with that threat for such a pivotal portion of her life, Juana actively participated in these movement organizing spaces to the best of her ability. This participation, primarily through mentorship, facilitated her role in transferring knowledge to these younger organizers through community knowledge–sharing practices. Describing her experience mentoring youth in the contemporary immigrant rights movement, Juana noted, "[At my university] a lot of our students are undocumented or are [members] of the 1.5 [generation]. So I take my mentorship very seriously, and I continue to [mentor students from campus organization name]. I do all of the panels that they ask me to be on, I do all of that institutional work to continue being visible as a grad[udate] student, that was kind of what I knew I could do."

For Juana, mentorship served as an important mechanism through which she both remained involved in the immigrant rights movement and worked to mentor and encourage subsequent generations of youth organizers. Students looked to Juana as an elder but also saw her as somewhat of an older sibling figure, pointing to the critical role of emotional labor that formerly undocumented women took part in. Juana's active efforts to maintain a visible presence within the movement were linked to her desire to continue building meaningful affective bonds with other movement participants. This relational trust and emotional support that Juana took part in through her mentorship of undocumented students at her university illustrate what legal scholar Kathryn Abrams has referred to as "reciprocal emotions," which can be understood as "the feelings that those who are mobilizing rights may experience for each other." Elaborating on the theoretical and practical importance of these emotional ties, she explains, "Sociologists of emotion have demonstrated the importance of bonds of trust and affection that run from members to leaders, as well as from members to each other, in motivating action and in fostering persistence within protest movements."[5] Abrams stresses that this is particularly important for "high-risk movements" in which the community in question may be especially vulnerable to attack. Undocumented immigrants, subject to deportation and other reprisals by the state for their organizing efforts, arguably constitute a high-risk movement.

These mentoring relationships that Juana developed with the undocumented students at her institution were also indicative of her desire to give back to others and continue supporting movement activism despite her increased workload as a graduate student. Though this heavier workload and additional commitments—teaching, traveling to conduct research, and so on—affected her capacity to organize, Juana did not allow these responsibilities to prevent her from remaining involved. Instead, she reshaped her involvement in the movement around these newly acquired responsibilities. In doing so, she assumed a greater role as a mentor that, in turn, included a great deal of emotional care work in her collective conversations and individual meetings with students.

Though Juana's role as a graduate student shifted the form of her involvement in the movement, she realized that this newfound identity was empowering, allowing her to share details about her educational trajectory with undocumented students who were interested in pursuing graduate study. Explaining what forms this type of mentorship took, Juana noted:

> I did [the] Dream Summer [Program] twice. I did it last summer and the summer after my first year. Same thing, you know, I'm like the only grad student in that space, so I put on panels about grad school, I talk to folks about grad school, I just try to find a way to find the undocumented students in whatever space I'm at. And try to do some demystifying work of the possibility of doing grad school. And then I teamed up with someone who is a really close friend of mine who's also another undocumented PhD student who graduated this year, and [with] her in STEM and me in the social sciences/humanities, we were holding it down for the panels, we were holding it down for anything that [the campus undocumented student organization] was asking us [to do].

As Juana's efforts to shed light on the graduate school admissions process make clear, in addition to the mentoring she provided for undocumented youth at her campus, she was also well situated to provide important career and educational advice. A more formal type of knowledge sharing than mentoring, participation in these panels and undocumented youth development spaces allowed Juana to work with younger generations of undocumented students both on a one-on-one basis and in a larger collective setting. Surprisingly, both instances of knowledge sharing underscored the importance of Juana's identity not necessarily as an undocumented or formerly undocumented individual but as a graduate student at her university. Access to such role models and mentors, Juana understood, was a unique experience; she later shared that finding such mentors while she was going through this process was a significant hurdle and almost discouraged her from attending graduate school in the first place. While not specifically an activist or movement organizing space, the mentorship conversations and relationships Juana developed with undocumented undergraduate students provided her a way as a formerly undocumented individual to continue engaging with members of the undocumented immigrant movement, in particular, the youth. In doing so, she assisted in cultivating knowledge transmission across age cohorts and working to support and build up the future generation of activists. It is not surprising that the college/university space was a generative one for social movement activism and intergenerational mentorship among cohorts of undocumented community members. A common thread in the DREAMer narrative that Walter Nicholls described in his book *The DREAMers* was undocumented youth's realization of their undocumented immigrant status when applying to college.[6] As I argued in the Introduction, undocumented youth are uniquely situated at the forefront of the contemporary immigrant rights movement due to their politicization in the US K-12 education system and the fact that many were able to attend college, which in turn served as a critical space for their political socialization.

In addition to more formal knowledge-sharing spaces such as Dream Summer Workshops and graduate school panels, Juana also participated in efforts to raise the political and oppositional consciousness of the young people with whom she worked through her role as a graduate student teaching assistant. Expanding upon how she utilized this role to teach students about the history and context leading to migration, especially undocumented migration, Juana explained:

> I [also] see and I appreciate my participation as a student in the way that I am contributing to the education movements and preparing students. I mean, today, for instance, . . . I'm teaching my own course and this week for the course we went over the [causes of] migration. So I delivered two

lectures, [one on] the . . . US intervention in the Caribbean and Central America. And a lot of my students don't know, they just don't know, and I'm like "what?" Some of the students are familiar with this history, with this political history, but a lot of them [are not]. So I see the importance of doing this work, and I see its activist, scholar-activist kind of aspects, but I wouldn't consider myself an activist. I'm still trying to figure that one out, to be honest. I am not organizing on the ground, or in legislative work. I guess I could say yes, yes . . . by all means, I'm participating in the consciousness shifting of some sort, and educating the next generation.

Similar to the community knowledge–sharing practices enacted by Asian undocumented organizers who intentionally drew upon the silenced narratives of Asian undocumented immigration and the undocuqueer activists who emphasized the appropriation of the "coming-out" strategy from queer communities, Juana's efforts to educate Latinx students about their history are critical to the movement's growth and success. By learning about their own community's histories, these young people are able to develop and cultivate not only a legal and political consciousness but also an oppositional consciousness. This oppositional consciousness, informed by the articulation of a nuanced historical narrative, in turn, allows these young people to take part in activism that is simultaneously targeted toward correcting historical injustice and importantly informed by movement campaigns, strategies, and approaches.

Nevertheless, as a graduate student, Juana has had to contend with the fact that she no longer can be as involved in movement organizing spaces given limitations on her time and her focus on advancing in her academic career. In her comment Juana draws a distinction between "legislative work" and the more education-focused, consciousness-raising efforts that she took part in through her teaching, coming to the conclusion that she "wouldn't consider [herself] an activist" and that it was something she was "still trying to figure out." The uncertainty over whether to label herself an activist is indicative of the multiple shifts that Juana underwent: from a formerly undocumented individual to a person with legal status in the United States, from an undergraduate to a graduate student, and from a movement "youth" to an "elder" in the community. The compounded effects of these experiences point to the need to examine the shifting nature of legal status, as well as the fluid nature of other social identities and experiences that undocumented youth organizers undergo as part of the life course, or what Roberto Gonzales views as the transition to illegality.[7] Building on Gonzales's concept, this example shows how the transition to illegality, for some, is followed by the transition to legality.

In contrast to Juana's experience as a graduate student mentor at a local university, Anna, a formerly undocumented organizer from Chicago, continued her involvement in movement organizations largely with the intent of assisting other movement activists as they worked through their own trauma as undocumented people in the United States. Anna accomplished this primarily via music workshops, which allowed her to serve as a mentor to individuals whom she referred to as "the next generation of immigrant rights leaders." In this process, Anna detailed how creating and engaging in musical performance facilitated her involvement in political activism and helped her share those experiences with peers in a manner that was not draining or exhausting emotionally:

> I was also making music and doing a lot of public community events with [group name] and [group name] based out of . . . Chicago. . . . Those experiences really taught me a lot. [At times] I felt like I wanted the world to empathize with my emotions but at the same time I was jarring myself by reliving these traumatic experiences for the world to be able to connect. . . . [But now] I feel through the art creation process . . . that is migrant centered, I've been able to find the most hope. . . . And I used my music to connect people to my story and my experience. And now the more that I study it, the more that I practice it, . . . I feel like there's these moments where I've been validated.

Affirming her own lived experiences and offering a readily accessible outlet for other undocumented community members to relate to, using music and music education to convey experiences and knowledge made dealing with traumatic and triggering experiences much more manageable for Anna. As we have seen in the earlier discussion of the scholarship on emotions, Anna's experience processing her own trauma from having lived for many years as an undocumented immigrant in the United States and in discussing those traumatic experiences with others, including other undocumented immigrant community members, was healing and therapeutic. Creating such a space, she explained, would hopefully enable others to take part in a similar process. This emotional work that Anna and her formerly undocumented immigrant women of color peers are taking part in, when working to mentor subsequent generations, is evidence of the enactment of emotional care work. In defining care work and its various manifestations as part of a largely feminized endeavor, sociologist Evelyn Nakano Glenn explains, "Caring can be defined most simply as the relationships and activities involved in maintaining people on a daily basis and intergenerationally. First, there is direct caring for the person, which includes physical care (e.g., feeding, bathing, grooming), emotional care (e.g. listening, talking, offering reassurance), and services to help people meet their physical and emotional needs."[8] The fact that, according to Nakano Glenn, emotional care is a key component of care work that individuals can provide for one another underscores the gravity of the work that Anna and her peers are undertaking. Seeing this care work as a mentoring and community-building endeavor, Anna points to the healing nature of music as a generative form of care work for herself and the young people with whom she interacts.

This less triggering and trauma-inducing medium and the collective aspect of music creation practiced by Anna and the youth she worked with also entailed efforts to correct dominant portrayals of undocumented communities. By working to correct these narratives, Anna and the youth sought to forge a space that allowed for authentic, transparent community building across different subgroups within the broader undocumented immigrant community. She explained:

> Undocumented art is beyond valid . . . it is one of the most relevant forms of art that is continually underfunded, and underrepresented and underrespected both in political organizations, but also in the wider spectrum of art and the world. Music has been my way of healing and feeling OK. . . . But at the same time it is so nourishing to be in [music creation] spaces. . . . It helps [us] go beyond political narratives and these kind of curated notions of our experience, these formulated and preconceived formats of delivering and sharing and connecting our experiences with

one another. And I don't mean to say that in a way that disregards the ways that organizations have [worked to spread various messages in the immigrant rights movement]. I understand the way and why [they did so] ... but I think [music] is a starting point and a powerful practice that people have used in the past, but I am also resonating with spaces that are going beyond [traditional narratives and messages].

Providing a means of, as Anna discussed, "go[ing] beyond political narratives," music offered a novel approach to engage this future genera-tion of undocumented youth as they collectively sought to recraft nar-ratives concerning their community members' everyday lives. Although Anna recognized the importance and necessity of the movement's focus on political campaigns and legislative wins, her enactment of commu-nity knowledge–sharing practices focused primarily on her emotional well-being and that of other movement organizers. Maintaining and prioritizing their collective well-being through art practice provided a means for her to bring the past and present into conversation similar to Juana's efforts in the college/university context. Through music, Anna was able to assist her fellow movement activists in a collective healing process regarding the trauma they faced as undocumented people. This healing included Anna as someone who was in the process of adjust-ing her status and was also recovering from these years of trauma and insecurity.

The healing process thus points to a key connection that undoc-umented and formerly undocumented organizers have been able to forge with one another despite their different legal statuses. This work also provided a means to build community in a way that was, as Anna noted, independent of the limited scripts and frameworks provided in mainstream political discourse. Anna's experience points out that ac-cess to legal status may in fact serve as a step toward the empowerment of undocumented community members, allowing individuals to con-tinue "coming out of the shadows" and to make certain rights claims that they may have not have been able to access. Yet, her experience also shows that the condition of illegality, or of having been an undoc-umented person for such an extended period of time has profound and enduring consequences for community members. Using the medium of music as a space for emotional processing, building connections with others in the immigrant rights community, and disseminating a community-centered message, Anna's example of her continued involvement in the immigrant rights movement while she was in the process of adjusting her immigration status illustrates the continued importance of the enactment of community knowledge–sharing processes between undocumented and formerly undocumented immigrant rights organizers.

As Juana's and Anna's narratives demonstrate, for formerly undocumented activists who have continued their involvement in the movement, their participation often focused on uplifting younger individuals who they saw as future movement leaders. These connections between these formerly undocumented immigrant women and members of this younger generation were largely developed by foregrounding other social identities these women held, including racial and gender identities. As a result, these women were able to transmit knowledge across generational divides and to draw on their own lived experiences and turn them into effective educational opportunities for furthering the development of the movement overall. Though some might assume that the immigration status of these formerly undocumented women would become less salient or potentially irrelevant, the examples of the women in this chapter demonstrate the importance of their multiple social identities, including their formerly undocumented status, in facilitating the mentorship of and investment in a future generation of undocumented youth organizers. Often occurring at the individual level, workshops like the ones Anna described provided an important creative and emotionally supportive outlet for undocumented and other marginalized youth to share their experiences and develop emotional bonds with one another in an undertaking that prioritizes the continued relevance of formerly undocumented immigrant activists' participation in movement activism.

Strategic Leveraging of an Intersectional Movement Identity: The Continued Participation of Formerly Undocumented Activists

In the multiple social movement organizing spaces that I observed and participated in while conducting fieldwork, a significant emphasis was placed on centering the needs and experiences of directly affected individuals. These individuals were often seen as having the largest stake in the conversation because they were personally affected by the outcome of the decisions made during those meetings and on behalf of the particular movement organization. At the beginning of my work in these spaces, it seemed that the process of centering these individuals' experiences and perspectives was relatively straightforward as it meant allowing undocumented people in the space to direct the conversation and related actions. Yet, as I continued my fieldwork, I noticed that greater numbers of undocumented individuals had recently adjusted their immigration status—either through marriage or by obtaining another form of legal relief—or were in the process of doing so. Consequently, the question of who constituted a "directly affected individual" became more complicated than I had initially anticipated and, as I soon discovered, as many of the activists in those spaces had also previously thought. As the narratives in this section demonstrate, not all formerly undocumented individuals experienced the process of adjustment of status in the same way, and many were at different stages in the process. This finding was reflected in how the formerly undocumented immigrant women of color activists explained their experiences with processes of self-identification, their relationship to the movement, and their impetus for continued participation in immigrant rights organizing. Seeing oneself occupying a space between directly affected individual and movement ally also facilitated formerly undocumented activists' exploration of other avenues through which they were able to participate in the movement and reflect on their intersectional identities.

In response to a question regarding which identity she saw as particularly salient in her daily life and how she approached her participation in the immigrant rights movement, Azucena, a formerly undocumented activist residing in the San Francisco Bay Area who at the time had not yet adjusted her immigration status, emphasized her indigenous identity. However, like her immigration status, her identity as an indigenous woman was also one that she shared selectively with those whom she trusted, and depending on her comfort level with the individual in question, she might share more or less about her indigenous background. Elaborating on this point, Azucena explained, "If I was to meet someone at this point in my life, I would identify myself as who I truly am, you know, an indigenous woman of [Mexico]. I feel sometimes it just really depends on who I'm talking to. So if I feel pretty comfortable with you, I'll be like 'yeah, I'm indigenous and I come from this specific pueblito.' This will usually trigger more conversation like, 'oh really?' and stuff like that."[9] Azucena's intersectional identity as an indigenous woman and undocumented immigrant shapes her sense of self and her interactions with those around her. Even within discussions of undocumented immigrant communities, as Azucena continued to remark, the visibility of indigenous women has been extremely limited. This limited treatment of indigenous identity in the undocumented context has in turn led Azucena to hesitate when sharing her indigenous identity and to do so most often situationally. Yet, Azucena's assertion of a strong indigenous identity alongside the other social identities that she holds underscores the relevance of these identities beyond solely their intersections with one's undocumented immigrant status. In terms of how she identities, Azucena offers a theorization of an identity that pushes beyond static notions of undocumented immigrant identity as solely related to one's immigration status. Also, though Azucena no longer identified as an undocumented person, she shared how the other social identities she held, irrespective of her undocumented status, continued to be extremely important in how she related to and interacted with others, in particular "directly affected" social movement participants. Thus, Azucena's emphasis on an intersectional identity, which she articulated during our first interview, prior to her adjustment of her immigration status, points to the key impact that activists' multiple social identities make across the spectrum of the various immigration statuses individuals may hold.

Azucena's initial identity as an undocumented person was not one-dimensional; rather, the process of adjusting her status allowed her to remain connected to her fellow movement participants through her other social identities, such as her identity as an indigenous person and a woman. Reflecting on how she is read and understood by others in the immigrant rights movement, in particular by directly affected individuals, and how she seeks to represent herself after having adjusted her immigration status, she explained:

> These [undocumented] young people [that I work with] are getting all kinds of messages from their friends, from the school, from the streets,

and so it can be difficult to have an impact on them. And so my experience as an undocumented student who went to [university name] and my
specific background as an indigenous person who grew up with limited
resources, in an impoverished family and with gang violence, domestic
violence and substance abuse [have all shaped how I relate to the young
people with whom I work and how they understand me].

As these remarks point out, even though Azucena previously identified as an undocumented individual, she shared and continues to share
additional identities with the young people whom she mentored. The
similarities and differences between Azucena's identities and those of
the youth she mentors were a topic that Azucena had to grapple with
prior to adjusting her status, and as a result, was one that she had already
taken time to reflect on and begun to navigate. After becoming a legal
permanent resident, Azucena still was able to draw upon her other
social identities—as a working-class individual, an immigrant, and a
person of color—to build rapport with the youth organizers she mentored. In addition, Azucena had earned respect from and established
common ground with these young people prior to adjusting her status;
thus, they saw her not only as an undocumented immigrant and mentor
but also as an individual holding a variety of social identities to which
they could relate.

Explaining how a primary way in which the youth saw her as different was due not to her shift in immigration status but rather to her education level, Azucena added: "Even though I went to [university name],
the [youth] don't view me as a nerdy person who went to [university
name]. [Instead], a lot of them see me as someone they can relate to and
share things with. This is because of my background and the way that I
carry myself . . . that's supercrucial and is a huge component in the work
that I do. I need to be relatable to these young people otherwise I become irrelevant, and if I become irrelevant then this work can't be done."
Because of Azucena's strongly rooted sense of self and her continued
emphasis on the importance of an intersectional framework for theorizing her own identity, she did not find her ability to relate to the youth
hampered or lessened during the process of adjusting her immigration
status and remaining involved in these immigrant organizing spaces.
Rather, Azucena extended her use of an intersectional framework by

reshaping her identity as a formerly undocumented person in a way that still emphasized her identity as an immigrant, but she also worked to be open and transparent with the young people she mentored regarding her new identity as a legal permanent resident. She remarked, "Some people still think that I [have] DACA maybe because I'm constantly not putting it out there [that have adjusted my immigration status through marriage]. But some people just assume that I have DACA and a travel permit. . . . The youth I work with do know though that I am an ally."

This intersectional approach to understanding and deploying her own identity served Azucena well in her work with organizers prior to her adjustment of status and afterward. It allowed Azucena to be fully transparent and open with the youth about the shift in her immigration status and to continue the critical work of mentoring a new generation of young people who will lead the movement forward. As her comments demonstrate, an individual's experience with immigration status is not fixed, but rather is fluid and continually shifting, even to the point at which an individual may no longer be undocumented. Keeping this in mind is vital to understanding the various social identities that movement activists have drawn upon in their efforts and their ability to continue to build a mobilized, collective base of participants to advance the movement's overall cause.

For Juana, the process of adjusting her immigration status allowed her to undergo substantial shifts in how she saw her own identity. Similar to Azucena, Juana emphasized the centrality of an intersectional identity with regard to how she understood her own lived experience prior to this shift in her immigration status. Yet, this shift allowed Juana to develop a broader, more capacious understanding of her intersectional identity and to consider its role in relation to how she navigated her continued participation in the immigrant rights movement. Describing her early participation in the movement, Juana stressed how it centered largely on her racial and gender identity as a Chicana due to the mentors and community with which she was surrounded: "OK, so it's interesting because when I was at [university name] I was . . . a Chicana. I had Chicana mentorship, women of color mentorship, my homies were like undocumented folks. At the time I was in a very, like, straight relationship, so my understanding of gender was very limited. And even the stuff I was engaged with I just didn't have enough frameworks to understand gender and sexuality in more complex ways. So that wasn't a huge part of my identity." For Juana, building community with other Chicanas and other undocumented women of color provided her with a strong support network of mentors and friends at the undergraduate institution she attended.[10] This focus on a Chicana identity, however, shifted for Juana during the process of entering a doctoral degree program and adjusting her immigration status. As she shared during our interview, this change in how she understood her identity caused her to question some of the assumptions present in Chicanismo. Such questions result from her interest in the liberatory politics of Chicanismo as a political ideology, but also its legacy as a framework for understanding Mexican/ Mexican American identity that focuses primarily on immigrant communities' experiences in the receiving country. Juana discussed how her identity became one that gravitated toward an emphasis on a transnational context, foregrounding an overarching immigrant identity. She explained:

> I'm [now] really reevaluating a lot of those [theoretical] frameworks of identity [I used to identify with] and [thinking about] how I relate to them [now]. So one, my status changed, which means that I have the ability to have a far more transnational experience. I think visiting family in Mexico and going to Mexico, my relationship with Mexico has shifted. I became way less nationalist and once I moved to [city], I began being conscious of my understanding of Chicanismo and really questioning it. Even in the way I understood myself as a Chicana shifted. And I think part of what shifted it was being in spaces with Central American folk and being conscious of folks' [diverse experiences], the cultural/political hegemony of Mexican-Americans in [city]. And the effects that it has with other Latino communities. So that really shifted my thinking around Chicanismo. So I don't really consider myself a Chicana. I consider myself an immigrant, I am someone who has had this immigrant experience and that's still very central and very important to me.

The shift that Juana underwent in terms of her own identity in reimagining of herself as a transnational subject is indicative of how identities are fluid and shift over time. While Juana's adjustment of her immigration status shifted her identity as an undocumented person in immigrant rights organizing spaces, she also underwent a transformation in terms of her understanding of her immigrant identity as constituting a transnational immigrant experience. This transnational immigrant experience was representative of, as Juana described, a desire to forge stronger ties with her homeland and to fully embrace the Mexican immigrant aspect of her identity.

Paradoxically, by gaining her permanent residency in the United States, Juana was able to embrace more fully her identity as a Mexican national, rather than needing to repeatedly emphasize her identity as a youth or as someone who had spent her adolescence in the United States. This transnational aspect of Juana's identity and her foregrounding of an immigrant identity blurred the boundary between directly affected and ally individual in the movement, leaving her somewhere in the middle. Yet, this repositioning also allowed her to become involved in more new and different movement spaces, as well as in spaces that facilitated exploration of other aspects of her identity as a Mexican citizen and as an immigrant in addition to her experience as a woman and a person of color.

High-Stakes Allyship: A Range of Experiences and Approaches

While much of the discussion in this chapter thus far has considered formerly undocumented immigrant women of color's experiences as allies and at times as directly affected individuals, an examination of the role of allyship, as both enacted and experienced by these women demonstrates the complex ways in which even the category of ally itself can be operationalized. In the contemporary immigrant rights movement, formerly undocumented women I interviewed were at various stages in the process of adjusting their status, as outlined in chapter 1. A lengthy and complex process, this has resulted, as I discuss in this section, in the formation of a continuum of experiences with and approaches to enacting high-stakes allyship in a social movement context. I begin with an examination of individuals who see themselves as allies and who, in actively operationalizing such an identity, have sought to make room for the voices of directly affected movement participants. This is supplemented by an analysis of activists who themselves rely on the support of their US citizen spouses in undergoing this process and still see themselves very much as directly affected movement participants. Building on the previous section's analysis of the blurred divide between movement participant and ally, this section ends with an overview of how the shift from an undocumented to a formerly undocumented individual, captured within the framework of high-stakes allyship, complicates an understanding of allyship and the various forms it may take.

The case of Azucena is emblematic of the experiences of individuals who shared how the shift in their classification by the federal government from undocumented immigrant to legal permanent resident caused them to view their relationship to immigrant rights movement activists within the scope of a traditional ally framework. In her new role as an ally, Azucena shared how she saw herself as an ally but knew that, because she had lived for so many years as an undocumented immigrant, she could be viewed by others as a high-stakes ally, or an individual with close personal and political ties to directly affected movement participants. She explained:

> I think now [that I have] a green card it gets a bit interesting because having that green card has given me that flexibility to . . . take a step back [from organizing] and say this may not be as urgent for me as it [was] before. . . . [My relationship to the movement has] changed in that if I was still in line for DACA and had a work permit, then the need to organize around it, and the need to be supervocal about it, would have been more pressing. . . . Because I don't rely on [DACA], I'm going to support [those who do], but I'm [also] going to take a backseat and let someone who is going through that trauma [having DACA taken away from them] take the lead. . . . Of course it concerns me because I work with members of this population and have family members who are affected by it, but I don't need to. . . . make my story be at the front of it.

Though Azucena has close ties to movement participants, having worked alongside them as a fellow undocumented organizer for many years, in her newfound conceptualization of her own identity as an ally, she now saw her role as one that supported and nurtured the political empowerment of current undocumented youth. In doing so, she sought to make space for new leadership among an up-and-coming generation of young people. Azucena's desire to make space for those directly affected individuals also points to her acute understanding of the movement's efforts to center these individuals' experiences and narratives. Her own lived experience helps her to understand the care and attention they need. Yet, as with many non–formerly undocumented individuals who engage in high-stakes allyship, this intimate understanding of the movement's priorities can also be gleaned in other ways, such as having a family member, close friend, or partner who is an undocumented individual.

While openly embracing her newfound positionality and consciously using the term "ally" to identify herself during our conversations, Azucena elaborated on how this shift in identity helped her to recognize the intergenerational differences in terms of how undocumented status is experienced among community members: "Even though I was an undocumented student a few years ago, I think . . . political climate[s] change and that needs to be acknowledged. And it's completely different time [today]. I can't be like as a formerly undocumented student [you must do this] . . . because the context is different. I think now I work to be a good ally and to allow those whose voices matter to speak up and share what they need to share about their experience." A strong, highly visible leader in the undocumented immigrant community, Azucena drew upon the sense of mutual trust that she had developed with other undocumented community members over the course of her involvement in the movement: prior to, during, and after the process of adjusting her immigration status. This work was also informed by her lived experience as a previously undocumented individual. Acknowledging that even within undocumented spaces political and legal circumstances change, Azucena was already actively thinking about the similarities and differences between her experiences and those of the youth with whom she worked. This enabled her to continue this process of reflection after adjusting her status.

Similarly, Luna, a formerly undocumented activist from Chicago who has remained involved in the immigrant rights movement since adjusting her immigration status, explained how she, too, saw herself as an ally rather than a directly affected movement participant. This shift was not necessarily easy to make; rather, it was part of a larger process of legally adjusting her immigration status and emotionally coming to terms with how this reshaped her participation in and relationship to those directly affected movement participants. Articulating the difficulty of this experience, Luna noted:

> I think that [my involvement in the immigrant rights movement] has changed in that . . . we [individuals who have adjusted their immigration status] check in with folks that are still directly impacted by whatever campaign or whatever it is that we are trying to do. So I feel like that's really important to do now and [for us organizers] not [to] get super caught up in like, well, I've been doing this for so long I know how to do it; this is just the way that we're gonna do it. I think for a lot of us, [even] those who have DACA . . . or [for those of us] who are now residents or citizens even, this is something that we struggle with because a lot of us are still, like, in that core [leadership] team, you know.

While Luna was now technically an ally of undocumented immigrants rather than a directly affected individual, she, like others interviewed in San Francisco and New York City, emphasized how having family members who were directly affected was a critical component of how she understood and experienced her new role as a movement ally. Luna added, "So the other reality too is that even though, for example, my [immigration] status changed, my parents and brother, you now, are still undocumented. So it's like how we come into this work [has changed] but [at the same time] recognizing that these experiences are still there [of having lived as undocumented immigrants for such a long period of time] and [these are] our family's struggles, you know." Maintaining one's active participation in the immigrant rights movement alongside directly affected individuals and being a trusted ally of these community members, as Azucena and Luna have done, are key to laying the groundwork of one's unique positionality as a high-stakes ally. At the same time, these formerly undocumented women all identified the importance of having undocumented family members and the role that these close kinship ties had in reminding them of the limitations of their newly acquired immigration status.

In comparison to the experiences of formerly undocumented women like Azucena and Luna, who consciously sought to assert an ally identity as a result of their shift in classification by the federal government, others still saw themselves as in a state of transition and, as such, continued to identify as directly affected movement participants. For example, Anna described how she relied on her partner, a US citizen, to encourage her to continue her participation in the immigrant rights movement during this difficult and challenging period in her life: "So my partner and I started dating before I went to the Philippines in 2015 and we got married last year . . . and he's just always been somebody that I trusted . . . somebody who was really honest and is a good listener. . . . And he's been truly supportive of me in every way. . . . He knows that [immigrant rights organizing] is my life's work and whenever I'm bummed out or feeling low . . . he's always really supportive."

As Anna's words highlight, the support of her US citizen spouse was critical to her ability to process the complex emotions encapsulated in the adjustment of status experience. She continued, "I think that at the same time he also recognizes how sometimes doing this work and how much it takes up space in your physical, emotional and your day to day . . . how it can be really hurtful. . . . And so . . . he is a really strong support system in my life that also has seen all the sides of my work." The emotional investment that Anna's partner provided also facilitated her participation in the immigrant rights movement with a focus on coalition building. Through her participation in movement organizing spaces, she sought to underscore for her fellow Asian immigrant community members the relationship between the immigrant rights movement and other social justice movements. Elaborating on this point she shared:

And people that see me in a Filipino context don't know about the migrant context necessarily. I think people kind of see certain parts of you and don't really know all that is you and your partner sometimes gets a bigger view of that. . . . And being in [organization name] and working with Asian American organizations I could literally and systemically see, feel, and read and recognize the barriers [to coalition building]. . . . I could see why my community wasn't even able to be present in specific conversations around antiblackness and conversations around immigrant rights, and I feel that experience helped me understand to be balanced . . . because it's easy to say my people do not care about immigrant rights. This is trauma, and I was dealing with that directly within my community and my family.

Though Anna understood herself to be a directly affected movement participant, her experience points to how, even during the process of adjusting one's status, one may benefit from the support of other high-stakes allies. Her articulation of how high-stakes allyship, or allyship among those with close personal ties and/or connections to a movement, is enacted focused primarily on the critical role of her US citizen partner's support in furthering her participation in the immigrant rights movement. Additionally, her partner's encouragement of Anna's political involvement and her work alongside fellow immigrant community members helped open up new ways of envisioning the potential of social movement activism by contributing to the development of her own political and oppositional consciousness.[11] Although her newly acquired legal status resulted in an important shift in Anna's ability to travel and to engage in different types of social movement activism, her experience underscores the limitations of a shift in legal status as fully detaching someone who lived such a significant portion of her life as an undocumented immigrant in the United States.

As the experiences of activists like Azucena, Luna, and Anna demonstrate, many models emerged for how formerly undocumented immigrants dealt with the implications of their newly acquired legal status, in particular as it related to their continued participation in immigrant rights movement organizing. These models, I argue, should not necessarily be viewed as being in tension with one another; rather, they can be viewed as pointing to the continuum of experiences incurred by this important shift both in activists' everyday lives and in shaping their approaches to political organizing.

Yet, while Azucena, Luna, and Anna described the effects of this shift and their affinity with or efforts to distance themselves from the label of being a directly affected movement participant, Juana shared how she viewed these experiences as indicative of a shift that the entire community of undocumented immigrant organizers had been undergoing. In explaining this shift, she noted:

> I don't think [this shift from being an undocumented to documented individual is] something that [causes] people . . . [to] see me differently or . . . treat me differently. I think this is something happening with many people [in the movement]. [Many people are] finding ways of adjusting

their status. For some of us that were DACA recipients [we] . . . were able to have some kind of legal entry [through advanced parole that later helped with our immigration cases]. And some of us took the route of marriage to adjust our status. So I'm not the only one. . . . I think if anything it's just the group of those who either because they had a pending application or through marriage [they] adjusted their status. So the [experience of having] papers . . . I don't know if it's like "Oh, you don't understand me [as an undocumented person] anymore [because you have papers]," or more like "good thing you found someone to marry!"

The community-wide conversation that Juana described related to the potential to adjust one's immigration status through marriage, reentry through DACA, or other mechanisms such as obtaining a U visa underscores how undocumented youth, as a collective community, are continuing to grapple with the ongoing implications of their undocumented status across the life course.[12] As these young people reach the end of adolescence and young adulthood, they are actively seeking alternative ways to adjust their status and continue on with their lives in the face of government inaction emblematic in the unsuccessful passage of the federal DREAM Act in 2010.[13] If passed, the legislation would have provided an important, but still limited, pathway for these young people to pursue US citizenship.

Elaborating on the sense of community that this collective conversation and related thought process have cultivated, Juana continued: "It's kind of like that one feeling [you know] when like all of us were competing for scholarships at [university name] and then we knew we were competing with each other but we still share[d] the info so we could all apply to it. . . . And then someone gets it and we're like yeah, yeah, great job. And we're like, you know, happy for each other. So I think at least for me, the people that I've surrounded myself with have been very . . . happy [that I was able to adjust my immigration status]." Surrounding herself with friends and other undocumented people who were similarly seeking to adjust their status, many of whom who had done so through marriage to a US citizen partner, demonstrates how the cases of Azucena, Anna, and Juana are not isolated instances but rather indicative of a broader shift taking place within the undocumented immigrant community. As these formerly undocumented women of color organizers work to (re)negotiate their relationship to the movement and its participants, they are also being confronted with questions about their own identities, their immigration status, and the role(s) they seek to fill in the movement. It is important to view these categories of directly affected movement participant and ally as being on a continuum, including the category of high-stakes ally. For instance, as Anna's experience has shown, even high-stakes allies themselves can require support from other high-stakes allies. Ultimately, undocumented immigrant organizers comprise a diverse and vibrant community of individuals who, at each step in the organizing process, reconsider the ways they can support one another and simultaneously reflect on the approaches and strategies they have thus far employed in their activism to advance the cause of increased rights for all immigrants.

Conclusion

As is clear from this chapter's discussion of formerly undocumented women who continued their participation in the immigrant rights movement after adjusting their immigration status, much can be learned from this group's unique positionality in relation to movement organizing and the strategies they employ. The chapter highlights these individuals' use of identity-based strategies, analyzed through the Identity Mobilization Framework, which allows us to examine this group's use of an intersectional movement identity and to draw comparisons regarding the ways that formerly undocumented women of color, like their Asian undocumented and undocuqueer counterparts, strategically and purposefully draw upon an intersectional identity in their activism. Relatedly, these activists' narratives point to the importance of understanding how these individuals also engage in the important work of coalition building with members of other marginalized groups, emphasizing these activists' identities as formerly undocumented individuals, women, and people of color but also as indigenous people, as Asian individuals, and as community leaders.

The coalitional focus of these individuals' work emphasizes the potential of identity-based strategies to be strategically and purposefully leveraged by social movement organizers to overcome the structural and political limitations of holding a socially stigmatized and legally marginalized identity such as undocumented immigrant status. While undocumented status has often been discussed with regard to the effects of being an undocumented immigrant in the United States today, the narratives of formerly undocumented activists' continued participation in the contemporary immigrant rights movement underscore the importance of the lingering effects of having resided in the United States as an undocumented immigrant during adolescence. Also, given the focus within the literature on the sociohistorically constructed nature of immigrant legal status, these activist narratives point to the need to consider the shift from being an undocumented immigrant to adjusting one's immigration status alongside activists' experiences with other socially constructed identities, which evolve over time: racial/ethnic identity and sexual orientation.

Conclusion

When I began work on this book examining the strategies and tactics that undocumented immigrant activists utilized in their formation of a national social movement, I was often asked, "How can undocumented immigrants, especially in the face of a hostile and uneven legal context, mobilize to secure increased rights?" From my own experience working alongside undocumented community members during college and the ethnographic fieldwork I conducted in San Francisco, Chicago, and New York City, I learned that these undocumented immigrant organizers possessed a great deal of knowledge regarding their rights as immigrants residing in the United States and about the US legal system. Some of this knowledge resulted from personal experience, some of it from work with other social justice movement campaigns, and some of it from coursework they had completed while in college. Collectively this knowledge provided the resources individuals who some might consider unlikely political organizers drew from in their transformation into an immensely powerful group of social movement activists. This is the story that this book tells.

Nevertheless, this story is not solely about the role of the law and the legal system but also focuses on the identities and experiences of activists themselves. In addition to the individual strength and perseverance of undocumented immigrant organizers, a key component of the organizing I witnessed was activists' strategic emphasis on the importance of an intersectional immigrant identity.[1] Such an identity was framed as a resource among movement activists, one that could subsequently be utilized to build coalitions with members of other similarly situated groups. As a result, activists leveraged the buy-in that these broader coalitions offered to challenge overarching legal and political barriers to organizing due to their status as undocumented individuals.

Over the course of this book, I have shown how members of three specific subgroups within the immigrant rights movement—Asian undocumented, undocuqueer, and formerly undocumented individuals—have drawn upon the use of an intersectional movement identity to promote intra- and intermovement solidarity and coalition building. Drawing on these activists' efforts, I developed what I call the Identity Mobilization Model, a theoretical framework for explaining how activists mobilize their individual identities, develop a structural critique of oppression, and work to liberate themselves and members of similarly situated groups from such oppression. This research provides additional complexity to previous discussions of undocumented immigrant identity and the "stigma of illegality" by analyzing the tools and processes through which activists have successfully counteracted the limiting effects of liminal legality for the purposes of forming a broad, inclusive social movement. While focusing on the immigrant movement in the contemporary period, this approach of working to build a broader political base and set of potential alliances holds particular importance for similarly situated communities for which precarious legal and political positioning poses a significant barrier to engaging in social movement activism.

Key Insights and Takeaways

Organizing While Undocumented is directly in conversation with academic theorizations of migrant illegality, social movement activism, and intersectionality. Extending discussions of scholars who have outlined the deleterious and often-lingering effects of migrant illegality in the lives of undocumented immigrant community members, this book illustrates the ways that directly affected movement activists have successfully contested such stigma through the deployment of an intersectional movement identity.[2] This identity and its use form the basis of the book's Identity Mobilization Model. Through a recognition of the multiple social identities that social movement activists hold and these identities' role in undocumented community members' engagement in political activism, this book makes the case for an intersectional identity as a form of a movement's collective identity. As such, it demonstrates how an intersectional collective identity in fact works to propel social movement activism forward rather than to curtail a movement's ability to galvanize a group of individuals around a shared identity to make a particular set of rights claims. An intersectional movement identity can thus function as a strong collective identity for social movement activism and facilitate coalition building across groups. Finally, acknowledging the historical and activist roots in the theorization of intersectionality, the book advances intersectional theories and frameworks by applying them to contemporary social movement activism—the political organizing of undocumented immigrant youth—detailing the specific work that intersectionality is doing for the movement. This work entails both accurately reflecting the lived experiences and identities of movement organizers and also offering a way for organizers to engage in a meaningful critique of structural oppression and to use their identities to take part in activism to dismantle the structures that perpetuate such inequality in the first place.

The Enduring Importance of an Intersectional Movement Identity in Theory and Practice

Since the time I conducted the initial fieldwork for this book, immigrant rights activists have continued to develop additional strategies and tactics in their social movement organizing. Such work has become increasingly important given the draconian approach to immigration enforcement that has been enacted since the election of Donald Trump as president of the United States in 2016. As part of these efforts, activists have continued to emphasize the centrality of an intersectional movement identity as a tool for overcoming legal barriers to activism. In doing so, I argue, they have also taken part in a process of envisioning new forms of intersectional identities and imagining additional coalitional possibilities with groups whose identities are also stigmatized and/or criminalized under the law.

As this book has shown, an examination of activists' use of an intersectional framework offers important implications for scholarship on immigration, social movements, and law. Yet the experiences of undocumented immigrant activists discussed here and the related strategies these activists deploy to fight for increased rights provide key insight for social movement activists today who seek to use an intersectional framework in their organizing. As such, these activist narratives point to the very real, tangible ways that an intersectional collective identity framework can lead to the formation of grassroots coalitions "on the ground." In light of the immense growth in immigration enforcement and policing at the federal and subfederal levels, I intend for the narratives in this book to provide a rich and inspiring history of the important work that activists have undertaken to date to encourage a future generation of activists working to advocate on behalf of undocumented immigrant and other similarly situated communities.[3] In doing so, I see this as dovetailing with the book's overarching focus on understanding the macro- and micro-level processes through which social change occurs by also providing tangible steps through which others might continue to take up the cause.

With the combined focus on scholarly and activist implications, in the next section I highlight three key examples of emerging articulations of an intersectional identity in the immigrant rights movement today: (1) the inclusion of African and Afro-Latinx individuals in undocumented immigrant narratives; (2) an emphasis on the importance of transgender individuals' narratives as part of the undocuqueer experience; and (3) expressions of solidarity with Muslim immigrant communities, especially during the Trump administration's imposition of the so-called travel ban. By offering these examples, I intend to illustrate the ongoing importance of utilizing an intersectional lens when examining contemporary social movement activism as enacted by members of legally and structurally stigmatized groups. Through the use of an Identity Mobilization Model framework, I gesture toward the ways that such an approach facilitates an understanding both of the role such an identity plays in the formation of an activist community and of its use as a tool for facilitating coalition building among seemingly distinct communities.

Undocublack Organizing: The Inclusion of Black Immigrant Narratives as Part of the Undocumented Immigrant Movement

Efforts to foreground the inclusion of African and Afro-Latinx immigrant narratives as part of the broader undocumented immigrant narrative are increasingly widespread and have come to occupy a more central position within the activism of undocumented immigrant communities today. This work has also entailed the creation of a specific space for self-identified black undocumented individuals to discuss their intersectional identities as both black individuals and undocumented immigrants. This approach recognizes the unique forms of violence that these individuals face resulting from the proliferation of racialized forms of violence against black bodies in the United States. Similarly, the liminality of these individuals' immigration status places them in an additionally precarious situation in which any encounters with law enforcement render them, like their fellow undocumented community members, at risk of deportation.

A leading national organization for black undocumented immigrant communities is the Black Alliance for Just Immigration (BAJI). According its website, the organization "was founded in April 2006 to respond to the massive outpouring of opposition of immigrants and their supporters to the repressive immigration bills then under consideration in the U.S. Congress." Moreover, the BAJI describes itself as an organization that "educates and engages African American and black immigrant communities to organize and advocate for racial, social and economic justice. . . . [It] provides training and technical assistance to partner organizations to develop leadership skills, works with faith communities to harness their prophetic voice and initiates vibrant dialogues with African Americans and black immigrants to discover more about race, our diverse identities, racism, migration and globalization."[4] With a dual focus on bridging African American and African diasporic communities, BAJI provides an opportunity for members of these two communities to collaborate and build bridges. As research has shown, African American and black immigrant community members undergo different experiences in terms of social mobility, educational access, and treatment in the US workforce.[5] At the same time, due to their identities as black individuals in the United States, they are often subject to similar forms of state surveillance and policing, regardless of their immigrant identities. More recently, however, a focus on the experiences of black undocumented individuals has highlighted the complex, nuanced nature of this identity.

Though there are always undoubtedly difficult, challenging conversations that must be had, the vibrant dialogues that spaces such as BAJI offer point to the potential that these efforts can have in creating a broad, unifying agenda for members of the immigrant rights community and members of similarly situated groups (in this case racial/ethnic minorities). These experiences with immigration status will undoubtedly vary across members of the African diaspora, but what these efforts make clear is an intentional focus on bridging difference to build coalitions and work toward the collective empowerment of black, black immigrant, and black undocumented communities. These processes follow the trajectory offered in the Identity Mobilization Model framework, taking a similar course to that of Asian undocumented communities, but in the context of a different set of racialization processes and historical legacies.

Incorporating Transgender Identities as an Important Constituency of the Undocuqueer Community

Chapter 3 discussed the role of undocuqueer—or undocumented and queer—activists in the immigrant rights movement, in particular these activists' role in leveraging their intersectional identities within both immigrant rights and queer activist spaces. While in the chapter I discuss transgender undocumented immigrant experiences as part of broader undocuqueer organizing efforts, since I initially conducted fieldwork for this project, conversations around the importance of including a transgender identity have continued to emerge. As the following example highlights, these efforts dovetailed with earlier work of self-identified undocuqueer organizers, underscoring the enduring resonance and importance of an intersectional identity in terms of affirming heterogeneity and illuminating opportunities to build coalitions with members of other marginalized groups.

Jennicet Gutierrez, a self-identified trans Latina activist, is a central leader within the immigrant rights and queer rights movements.[6] A core member of the organization Familia: Trans Queer Liberation Movement, Jennicet took part in an action in which she interrupted President Barack Obama at a White House Pride Celebration.[7] Jennicet's action at the White House is important because it not only illustrated the tension between different aspects of the queer community but also demonstrated the importance of solidarity among all members of the undocuqueer community.

The 2015 White House Pride Celebration began with introductory remarks by President Obama affirming the importance of "LGBTQ civil rights" alongside civil rights for all Americans. As part of this celebration, the president's staff members had invited prominent members of the undocuqueer community to attend. Near the beginning of the president's remarks, Jennicet, from the back of the crowd, exclaimed, "President Obama, release all LGBTQ [prisoners in] detention centers. . . . As a trans woman I am tired of the violence we are facing. Not one more deportation. Not one more deportation. . . . President Obama, release all LGBT . . . stop the abuse."[8] Fellow attendees then proceeded to shush Jennicet, who demanded that the Obama administration end the detention and abuse of LGBTQ immigrants in detention centers. In doing so, they told her, "This is not for you," rendering the experiences of trans undocumented women of color as outside a nationalist framework of including LGBTQ rights or what scholars in the field would term a homonationalist discourse.[9]

Making visible the voices of trans-identified undocumented immigrant individuals, Jennicet's action demonstrates the "double-edged sword" nature of an intersectional framework. While activists' efforts to foreground an intersectional undocuqueer identity allow for a more inclusive, nuanced understanding of undocumented immigrant identity, such an approach may also allow for an oversight of more subtle forms of difference within these broader categories as is the case in this example. Disidentifiying with notions of a queer identity that do not take into account transgender individuals' lived experiences, the efforts of Jennicet and other self-identified transgender undocumented immigrant activists point to the community's own challenges in working to expand the notion of an undocuqueer identity as one that also includes transgender community members' experiences. The ongoing struggle and contestation of how these categories are continually (re)made as a result of their operationalization point to the importance of examining the processes and mechanisms through which they are formed and deployed.

Moreover, Jennicet's interruption of President Obama was also somewhat reminiscent of Ju Hong's interruption of the president in November 2013 during a speech he made in San Francisco, hosted in the city's Chinatown neighborhood on the topic of immigration reform.[10] Ju, a self-identified Korean undocumented immigrant who was raised in the San Francisco Bay Area, stated, "Mr. President please use your executive order to halt deportations for all [the] 11.5 million undocumented immigrants [in] this country right now. . . . You have the power to stop the deportation for all 11.5 million," followed by other activists in the audience chanting, "Stop deportations, stop deportations." A key difference, though, was that when Ju interrupted President Obama, he was not removed from the stage but instead was allowed to remain and received a reply from the president, unlike Jennicet, who was shushed and then removed by the president's staff members. Moreover, Jennicet's adoption of a strategy that was previously put into practice by organizer Ju Hong illustrates the importance of examining the specific strategies developed by activists to strategically leverage an intersectional framework in ways that simultaneously promote inclusion and work to critique a politics-of-deservingness framework. This critique is enacted in a manner that works to expand the term "undocuqueer" to include other queer individuals who are not complicit in the perpetuation of a state agenda or a homonationalist perspective. Instead, the term undocuqueer is broadened to encompass the voices and experiences of dissenting undocuqueer individuals, in this case, trans undocumented activists.

"No Ban, No Wall": Forging a Coalition to Advocate for Both Muslim Immigrant and Undocumented Immigrant Rights

When Donald Trump was elected president of the United States in November 2016, his remarks along the campaign trail caused many members of the immigrant community across the country to be deeply concerned regarding the future of the Deferred Action for Early Childhood Arrivals (DACA) program, and rightly so.[11] Although the Trump administration announced the end of the DACA program on September 5, 2017, the question of whether the federal government had the legal authority to abruptly end the program is still under review in the courts.[12] Simultaneously, in the months leading up to the Trump administration's announcement ending DACA, an executive order commonly referred to as the "Muslim ban" (a ban against citizens from specific countries, including the majority of citizens from Iran, Libya, Syria, Yemen, Somalia, Chad, and North Korea, as well as some citizens of Venezuela, entering the United States) was announced. Restrictions under the ban vary from individuals not being allowed to immigrate to the United States whatsoever to being allowed to visit with additional screening or an added wait time. But the ultimate effect is that it significantly curtails and, in some instances, prevents citizens of these particular nations from entering the United States.[13] The Trump administration's third version of the travel ban, which was current at the time of the writing of this book, has been contested in ways similar to activists' efforts to prevent the Trump administration from ending the DACA program.

Both of these instances, the Trump administration's ending of the DACA program and the enactment of the Muslim ban, highlight how these issues exist at the nexus of government surveillance and efforts to increase detention of migrant communities. Such intentions were also not lost on organizers who developed the chant "No Ban, No Wall." Through this chant and in subsequent conversations, activists drew clear connections between the exclusion of primarily Muslim potential immigrants and visitors and the increasingly criminalized nature of immigrant detention in the United States. As part of maintaining the vulnerability and precarity of being an undocumented immigrant in the United States, any form of legal protections or rights-granting policies, such as DACA, must be stripped away. Given the distinct yet interrelated histories of these forms of oppression—heightened assaults on Muslim immigrants began after 9/11, and the mistreatment of Mexican and other undocumented immigrant communities as tied to larger historical narratives of Asian and Latin American immigrants being subjected to harsher immigration restriction/controls—one might assume that this would lead to a division between these two communities at they worked to counteract the marginalization and state-sanctioned oppression they were facing. However, in my continued collaboration and discussions with undocumented activists, they emphasized the importance of understanding the experiences of all immigrant and marginalized peoples as interconnected. By understanding their own intersectional identities as racialized communities of color and undocumented or partially documented individuals in the eyes of the US legal system, these communities were able to extrapolate from their individual political identities to form a collective group identity that could be leveraged in their organizing. By using the lens of the Identity Mobilization Model, one can interpret the role of these communities' intersectional lived experiences and identities in facilitating the inclusion of multiple groups to act upon the overlapping interests they share as targets of the state. Though these conversations remain ongoing, the development of a collective chant, showing up in solidarity for one another's events, and incorporating one another's critique of the US nation-state are mechanisms through which intersectional lived experiences, as this book has demonstrated, shape the potential for the continued proliferation of social movement efforts in the future.

Final Thoughts

In *Organizing While Undocumented*, I have highlighted the strength and resilience of undocumented immigrant communities today as exhibited by activists operating in a hostile legal and political context. While this context has shifted over time, including developments supporting and curtailing the rights of undocumented community members, these migrants' experiences with the "stigma of illegality" have endured. Drawing on extensive ethnographic fieldwork and in-depth interviews conducted with members of three of the movement's subgroups—Asian undocumented, undocuqueer, and formerly undocumented individuals—I highlighted the importance of an intersectional movement identity both internally and externally for activists in the contemporary period. The Identity Mobilization Model, which is this book's central organizing framework and primary theoretical intervention, can be used to analyze the strategies and tactics engaged by members of various groups that experience state-sanctioned marginalization and violence.

As I have discussed in this conclusion, such a framework for activism endures moving forward, as do the movement's future development and innovation. Through emerging conversations on black undocumented immigrant experiences, transgender undocumented immigrant narratives, and the nexus of efforts to combat Islamophobia and the criminalization of undocumented immigrant communities, activists have pointed to a commitment to an intersectional framework for engaging in social movement organizing. Rather than detract from the movement's ability to form and operationalize a collective identity, these multifaceted articulations of an intersectional movement identity point to organizers' ability to forge strategic and purposeful coalitions with members of other similarly situated groups.

Given that a primary force in securing increased rights for members of the undocumented immigrant community has been the political activism of undocumented immigrants themselves, I end this book with a renewed call for the active support of organizers who identify as directly affected individuals. These individuals' leadership and activism is often oriented around advancing a community-driven and community-centered agenda, and these individuals are those who will ensure that community needs are acted upon once they are realized in the form of legislation or other institutionalized forms. Thus, it is vital to support the work of these directly affected activists, and to allow them to take the lead in the creation of a future in which the structures that perpetuate inequity can be dismantled and the self-determination of community members can be fully realized.

ACKNOWLEDGMENTS

I am indebted to many individuals who have helped make this book possible and encouraged me along the way. First, I would like to express my deepest gratitude and thanks to the activists in San Francisco, Chicago, and New York City who generously shared their experiences and allowed me to come alongside them all as part of their work in the immigrant rights movement. Your courage and strength are beyond compare, and I have learned a great deal from your commitment to activism and your inspiring persistence in safeguarding the rights of your fellow community members. Now, as I work with immigrant rights organizers in my new home in Rhode Island, I repeatedly find myself drawing on the lessons I learned while working with you.

At NYU Press it has been a pleasure to work with Ilene Kalish, Sonia Tsuruoka, Mar Arain, and Alexia Traganas, who have helped shepherd this book through the review and revision processes. As a first-time author, I was extremely grateful to work with a team who believed in the work and its ability to make an important contribution to contemporary public debates on immigration, citizenship, and belonging. I am also grateful to the two anonymous peer reviewers who provided very helpful feedback that was instrumental to the revision process.

I remember spring 2015, as I was approaching my last set of law school finals, when Vice President for Institutional Diversity and Equity Liza Cariaga-Lo notified me that I had received a Presidential Diversity Postdoctoral Fellowship in the Department of American Studies at Brown University. Coming to Brown, I was generously provided with two key resources—time and mentorship—to develop the book manuscript. I am indebted to Liza for her guidance, support, and encouragement during my fellowship on campus. Thank you also to my fellow postdocs—Maria Abascal, Emma Amador, Stefano Bloch, Nicole Burrowes, Jordan Camp, Colleen Kim Daniher, Vanessa Fabien, Mariaelena Huambachano, Ryan Mann-Hamilton, Yalidy Matos, Sara Matthiesen,

Diego Millan, Anthony Pratcher II, and Iris Montero Sobrevilla—for the warm and supportive community you all created.

Having continued at Brown, now as an assistant professor, I am appreciative of the vibrant and dynamic community of American studies and ethnic studies faculty. Thank you to department chair Matt Guterl and to colleagues Bob Lee, Evelyn Hu-DeHart, Monica Muñoz Martinez, Daniel Kim, Ralph Rodriguez, Susan Smulyan, Leticia Alvarado, Liz Hoover, Adrienne Keene, Debbie Weinstein, Naoko Shibusawa, Elena Shih, Sandy Zipp, Kiri Miller, Beverly Haviland, Steve Lubar, and Rich Meckel. You all have provided a welcoming and supportive community for me to develop my scholarship and to put this research into practice. Outside of my department I have benefited from the support and advice of Faiz Ahmed, Paja Faudree, Françoise Hamlin, José Itzigsohn, Michael Kennedy, Jessa Leinaweaver, Brian Meeks, Tricia Rose, Susan Short, Richard Snyder, Zhenchao Qian, and Hye-Sook Wang. Andrea Flores, David Rangel, Adrienne Keene, and Christina "V" Villareal were participants in a junior faculty writing group that helped hold me accountable to the deadlines I had set for myself and also provided thoughtful encouragement along the way. Thanks also to weekday afternoon writing group members and fellow immigration scholars Almita Miranda, Lynette Arnold, and Dario Valles for the writing company.

Four specific individuals at Brown have provided immense support in the development of the manuscript, facilitating its transformation into a book. Evelyn Hu-DeHart served as a key mentor, frequently checking on my progress and generously reading over multiple drafts of individual chapters. José Itzigsohn also read multiple chapters and took time to explain his feedback to me during meetings at local coffee shops and via e-mail. Tricia Rose invited me to become part of the Center for the Study of Race and Ethnicity in the America's Fellows Seminar from 2015 to 2017, which was also a space where I was able to workshop individual chapters from the project and receive very helpful feedback. Ralph Rodriguez spent multiple hours at a local coffee shop on a spring weekend to talk through the structure and argument of the book, which ended up greatly improving its flow and structure.

This book also benefited from a daylong book workshop held at Brown University in fall 2018. Thank you to Shontay Delalue, Vice President for Institutional Diversity and Inclusion, and Matt Guterl,

Chair of the Department of American Studies, for the financial support that made this workshop possible. I am also grateful to Kara Cebulko and Roberto G. Gonzales, who read and discussed at length a full draft, providing insightful feedback on ways to strengthen and further develop the book. Walter Nicholls participated by sending his comments beforehand. An earlier version of chapter 1 benefited from comments from participants at the University of Houston Law Center's Institute for Higher Education Law and Governance Roundtable in May 2017. Thank you to Michael Olivas, who convened the roundtable, for his highly insightful comments on the chapter and his support in the development of the overall book. Thanks also to the other roundtable participants—Lara Badke, Michael Hevel, and David Nguyen—and to the roundtable's two other senior faculty mentors, Amy Gajda and Leland Ware.

University funding and course releases at Brown provided me with additional time to work on revisions and conduct follow-up interviews for the project. Thank you to the Dean of Faculty, Kevin McLaughlin, who provided course releases during my first year on the tenure track; Provost Richard Locke, who provided supplementary research funding during the second year of my postdoctoral fellowship; and Shontay Delalue and Matthew Guterl, who funded my participation in the National Center for Faculty Development and Diversity Faculty Success Program.

Prior to arriving at Brown, I enjoyed two years as a Gaius Charles Bolin Fellow at Williams College, where I developed many of the ideas for this book and reframed them after conducting additional fieldwork. At Williams, Carmen Whalen, Ondine Chavoya, Merida Rúa, María Elena Cepeda, Jacqueline Hidalgo, Gail Newman, Armando Vargas, and Molly Magavern were instrumental in facilitating my transition from a graduate student to postdoctoral scholar. Thanks to Scott Wong, Mark Reinhardt, Antonia Foias, Olga Schevchenko, Pia Kohler, Sara LaLumina, Rashida Braggs, and Gregory Mitchell for the guidance, mentorship, and community you provided during my time in the Berkshires. I am also grateful to Hannah Noel and Daniela Pila for friendship and writing accountability.

At UC Berkeley, I was lucky enough to be mentored by prolific scholars who also saw the importance of scholarship having a broader social justice–oriented impact. Evelyn Nakano Glenn was and continues to be an inspirational mentor who models what scholar activism looks like in her own work. Michael Omi pushed me to refine the arguments I developed in my writing and to be thorough and comprehensive in my work. Catherine (KT) Albiston introduced me to the field of sociolegal studies and helped me see the connections between the questions I was asking and those that animate this unique, interdisciplinary field of socio-legal studies research. Kathryn Abrams, Irene Bloemraad, Catherine Ceniza Choy, Lisa García-Bedolla, Elaine Kim, Ian Haney-López, and Leti Volpp all helped guide me during the formation of my research interests and the development of this project. During my undergraduate career at UCLA, where I majored in Chicana/o studies and first became interested in instances of coalition building and social movement activism, Robert Chao Romero, David Hernández, and Abel Valenzuela Jr. were extremely insightful and supportive mentors who encouraged me to consider the pursuit of a PhD and incidentally helped plant the seed for this project in its earliest form. Thanks to Nancy Guarneros, a fellow UCLA graduate, for her suggestion for the book's title during a panel at the University of Idaho School of Law in fall 2012.

I am indebted to colleagues writing on the topic of immigrant rights whose scholarship has helped shape my perspectives and who have been supportive of my approach to the issue. These individuals include Leisy Abrego, Abigail Andrews, Sofya Aptekar, Rick Baldoz, Lee Bebout, Irene Bloemraad, Edelina Burciaga, Alicia Schmidt Camacho, Kara Cebulko, Monisha Das Gupta, Marjorie Faulstich Orellana, Ruth Gomberg-Muñoz, Roberto G. Gonzales, Nadia Y. Kim, Lisa M. Martinez, Sofian Merabet, Hiroshi Motomura, Genevieve Negrón-Gonzales, Amalia Pallares, Marcel Paret, Joanna Perez, Heidy Sarabia, Nitasha Sharma, Matthew Shaw, Sarah Song, Ester Trujillo, Carolina Valdivia, Leti Volpp, Chris Zepeda-Millán, and Arely Zimmerman.

Funding for the research that laid the foundation for this book was provided by Brown University, Williams College, the National Science Foundation's Law and Social Science Program, the University of California Institute for Mexico and the United States, the UC Berkeley Center for Law and Society, and the UC Berkeley Department of Ethnic Studies. The American Bar Foundation in Chicago was extremely generous in providing office space and a vibrant scholarly community for me to undertake critical moments of the writing process. Thank you especially to Ajay Mehrotra, Jothie Rajah, Robert Nelson, Terence Halliday, and Laura Beth Nielsen. The New England Consortium of Latina/o Studies provided a home for an Asian-Latinx scholar from California looking for a group of individuals researching similar topics and many of whom also hailed from outside the region.

During the revision process I also benefited from the support of multiple individuals. Sarah Trayers provided key research support as a graduate research assistant for the project. Tina Park assisted with the creation of the tables for the book. Cynthia Gwynne Yaudes read over multiple drafts, assisting with the editing process to ensure clarity of ideas and flow.

This book is dedicated to my family: my parents, Gualberto and Thanh Ha, and my younger brother, Egan. It is also dedicated to my grandparents, Juan Escudero Bravo and Valeriana Coca Vega on my father's side and Lam Ky Phuc and Lam Thi Day on my mother's side. My family's stories of coming to the United States as refugees and as immigrants inspired me to look closely at the experiences of other immigrant communities. Through their lives I came to intimately understand the role of legal status on migrant and refugee community members' lived experiences and to develop a cultural sensitivity for the topic that, while I did not know it at the time, helped me conduct the research for this project in the first place. My family has also served as a persistent reminder, during the many years it took to conduct the research and writing of this book, of the importance of amplifying the voices of refugees and immigrants whose daily realities I seek to foreground in this work.

APPENDIX A

TABLE A.1. Descriptive Statistics of Interviewees

	Mean or Proportion		
	Total (*n* = 51)	Female (*n* = 29)	Male (*n* = 22)
Age			
Average age in years	24.4	24.5	24.4
Age range in years	19–32	19–29	21–32
Self-Identified Race[a]			
Asian or Asian American	27.5%	24.1%	31.8%
Latinx	76.5%	75.9%	77.3%
Self-Identified Sexual Orientation			
Queer/LGBTQ+	27.5%	20.7%	36.4%
Region of Residence			
Chicago Area	45.1%	44.8%	45.5%
New York City Area	13.7%	17.2%	9.1%
San Francisco Bay Area	41.2%	37.9%	45.5%
Highest Level of Education at Time of Initial Interview			
High school diploma	2.0%	—	4.5%
Associate degree	2.0%	—	4.5%
Bachelor's degree	74.5%	79.3%	68.2%
Master's degree	17.6%	17.2%	18.2%
JD (law degree)	3.9%	3.4%	4.5%
Country of Nationality			
China	3.9%	3.4%	4.5%
Colombia	2.0%	3.4%	—
El Salvador	2.0%	3.4%	—
Mexico	68.6%	65.5%	72.7%
Peru	3.9%	3.4%	4.5%
Philippines	13.7%	17.2%	9.1%
South Korea	2.0%	—	4.5%
Thailand	2.0%	—	4.5%
Vietnam	2.0%	3.4%	—

a The sum of the percentages may exceed 100 due to selection of multiple racial categories through self-identification by interviewee.

APPENDIX B

Methodological Notes

CONDUCTING INTERVIEWS AND INTERPRETING THE DATA

In-depth interviews for this book lasted from 1.5 to 2 hours and were conducted in a private location, often the offices of a local immigrant rights organization, but occasionally at a coffee shop or at the interviewee's workplace if they so desired. During a handful of instances, interviews were conducted over Skype when participants were unavailable to meet at other times and/or I was traveling to attend academic conferences.

Questions for the interviews covered a variety of topics, beginning with a discussion of the interviewee's immigration narrative—how and why they came to the United States, if they came with other family members, under what circumstances they came, and what their experiences were like once living in the United States. We then shifted to questions about individuals' experience within the education system—attending high school as undocumented students, barriers/challenges they may have faced in applying to college, and their experiences in technical school, college, and/or graduate school, if they attended. The last segment of the interview then focused on the interviewee's participation in the immigrant rights movement. Oftentimes individuals described their initial introduction to organizing occurring through their engagement with other causes that were not specifically related to their immigration status. On the other hand, given that the DREAM Act was introduced in 2001 and subsequently each year or so thereafter, many participants also shared how they worked on the passage of in-state tuition bills in their home states, building on the momentum of DREAM Act advocacy efforts.

I recorded interviews and later either transcribed them myself or had them transcribed by two undergraduate student research assistants. After the interviews were transcribed, I listened to the audio recordings while following along with the transcript to ensure accuracy and to note any shifts in tone and language. Per the university's Institutional Review Board policy, I deleted the audio files after transcription to ensure the anonymity of participants in case the data was ever subpoenaed, potentially placing the research participant at increased risk of being identified. While the majority of interviews were audio recorded, there were five interviews that I was unable to record and for which I instead took notes by hand.

After the transcriptions had been completed, I read through a few interview transcripts and coded them to identify key themes. With these emergent themes in mind, I then read through all the interviews, one region at a time (San Francisco, Chicago, and New York City), coding them as I went. I then compared themes from each site, developing macro-level themes across the three cities/regions. These were helpful in comparing across sites and developing the intersectional identity theme, which laid the foundation for the Identity Mobilization Model. After completing the coding process, I conducted follow-up interviews with some participants if there were any gaps or additional questions that emerged regarding themes for which I did not yet have enough information to draw a conclusion. I then coded these follow-up interviews using the same approach I employed during the first round of data collection to look for additional potential emergent themes among the interview data.

COMMUNITY ENTRÉE, RESEARCHER POSITIONALITY, AND AN EFFORT TO ENACT A COMMUNITY-BASED RESEARCH JUSTICE APPROACH

"Who are you and why are you interested in my life?" is a question I was repeatedly asked, subtly and in many different forms, throughout the course of researching this book. This question is one I would have likely asked if I met someone who was participating in a movement and asking many questions about an issue that did not necessarily affect them personally. While at first this question made me feel a bit uncomfortable, with time, on my motivations for conducting this research and it helped me reflect gradually developed a thoughtful answer to explain why I cared so deeply about the issue. My answer usually began with my identity and positionality as the son of a Vietnamese/Cambodian refugee mother and Bolivian immigrant father, and raised in Southern

California. I then explained how I attended college with several undocumented immigrant peers from whom I learned about the issue. It was
largely through these friendships as a college student that I was introduced to the impacts of undocumented status on a young person's daily
life and the immigrant rights organizing spaces in which they participated. While growing up, I had extended family members who were
undocumented, and as a child I was not able to fully grasp how this
shaped multiple aspects of their daily lives; I only heard secondhand,
from other relatives, of the difficulties they faced. Learning from my
friends and peers in college was transformative for me in terms of recognizing the critical importance of legal status as an axis upon which
marginalization occurs and is reproduced. Acknowledging the impact of
my positionality and relation to the immigrant rights movement helped
me to build trust with undocumented immigrant activists because it
established a sense of mutual understanding and commitment to the
issue—demonstrating not only my academic interest in the issue but
also my experience being raised by immigrant parents, familiarity with
individuals in my own community who were undocumented, and listening as I grew up to family conversations about our relatives' precarious
immigration statuses.

Moreover, as an individual who strives to put into practice a commitment of scholar activism, a term with contested origins, but which
Jennifer Bickham Mendez has described as referring to individuals who
work to "reconfigure knowledge production so as to shift power and
control into the hands of the oppressed or marginalized, privileging
'subjugated knowledges,'" I am profoundly aware of the importance of
coming alongside movements as an academic and, in doing so, working to redistribute power.[1] There are particular moments, however,
when showing one's support as a scholar-activist draws on our scholarly
identities as researchers and our activist identities as individuals seeking to accompany activists on this journey. As anthropologist Charles
R. Hale notes, an activist scholarship approach to conducting research
often complements traditional approaches to qualitative social science
scholarship. He writes, "Activist research and scholarship also . . . makes
explicit the tension in much traditional thought between 'really participating' and 'just observing,' especially in settings where social conflicts
and struggles shape what participating can mean. . . . [It] also empha-

sizes a kind of reflexivity about the conditions for formulating knowledge of different kinds."[2] Given my own scholar-activist commitments and the ethnographic approach I took in conducting research for this book, I interweave my experiences and reflections throughout various moments in the text. I do this not because I sought to draw attention away from the experiences of the activists with whom I worked. Instead, as part of my goal of highlighting the strategic decisions and thought processes present in movement organizing spaces, I wanted to be transparent regarding my own positionality as a researcher. By combining the voices of individual activists with analysis of my own, I aim to provide readers with a holistic perspective regarding what it was like to be part of the movement at this moment in time.

RESEARCHING A "HIGHLY RESEARCHED" COMMUNITY

Toward the conclusion of this project, the issue of undocumented immigration had significantly grown in popularity as a topic for researchers and in the overall political sphere.[3] As a result, a central issue I encountered working with members of this community was the question of how to continue building the trust I had already cultivated with organizers while recognizing that they would rightfully be concerned about the invasiveness of academics within their movement. Reaching out to organizers at the beginning of my project, I did so largely through networks I had established based on relationships from my home state of California that I had developed while I was an undergraduate student involved in local-level immigrant rights activism. In my continued work and research with undocumented community members, I sought to approach the research more as a partnership as opposed to a process of conducting research on a particular issue about which these individuals just happened to have in-depth knowledge. Shifting the power relationship and working with grassroots community-based organizations in the research process was a way that I sought to engage in research as part of an ongoing conversation that was attentive to community needs and desires.

Recognizing the increased popularity of this topic for researchers, I revised my interview protocol partway through the research process to incorporate questions for activists about their interactions with academic researchers. As Margarita, an undocumented student at a large public university in California, explained, "We [undocumented youth] have been researched a lot. All the time there are professors and grad students asking us about our lives. I don't mind it, but sometimes they don't realize that we are students and have things we need to get done. They act like we can just drop everything so that they can get the last-minute data they need for a paper, you know." Naming the highly researched nature of undocumented immigrant activism and its development into something that is now popular among researchers, Margarita's comments also point to the potential drawbacks of scholarly visibility. She continued, "The topic of 'DREAMers' has become so widespread that most people know something about our movement or at least heard of us. That wasn't the way it happened when we first started organizing. I remember when we didn't yet have national organizations working on this issue. But people need to understand that for us, this is our daily lives that we are talking about; it's not just research." Naming the stakes of research for members of the undocumented community, Margarita's comments also illuminate the importance of what it means for those individuals who are directly affected by an issue to speak for themselves. Rather than working to "give voice" to an issue, in this book I strive to center the voices and experiences of undocumented immigrant youth organizers. I see these efforts as contributing to an overall intervention in the knowledge production process wherein particular knowledges, such as those of scholars of color, let alone queer individuals and undocumented people, are often undervalued and overlooked, what education scholars Dolores Delgado Bernal and Octavio Villalpando refer to as the "apartheid of knowledge."[4] By foregrounding these knowledges and perspectives in the community members' own words, the narratives included in this book are meant both to be representative of particular strategies that activists have employed and to provide an important snapshot of the deliberations that have gone into the choices organizers have made.

NOTES

INTRODUCTION

1 García Bedolla, Nakano Glenn, and Escudero, "Working Together to Improve Campus Climate for AB540 Undocumented Students at UC Berkeley." From 2011 to 2012, I served as a graduate student researcher for the project "Working Together to Improve Campus Climate for Undocumented AB540 Students at UC Berkeley," led by co–principal investigators Professors Evelyn Nakano Glenn and Lisa García Bedolla. With their agreement, I supplemented their interview questions with my own questions as part of the data collection process for this book. We agreed that quoted passages that were responses to their project's questions would be used in the production of a joint Center for Race and Gender (CRG) and Center for Latino Policy Research (CLPR) research report, which was published in February 2013, and those in response to my supplemental questions would be for my exclusive use. All quotations in this book from San Francisco Bay Area partici-pants, except as noted, are drawn from responses to my supplemental questions or to the follow-up interviews that I conducted independently. The exceptions, noted in the text, include some quoted passages from their research project that I include to provide additional context to the respondent's narrative included in the book. Participants' responses that are taken from the Nakano Glenn and García Bedolla project are distinguished by an endnote citing the research report, coauthored by Evelyn Nakano Glenn, Lisa García Bedolla, and myself.

2 Hill Collins and Bilge, *Intersectionality*.

3 Passel and Cohn, "Unauthorized Immigrant Population."

4 Rumbaut, "Generation 1.5, Educational Experiences of."

5 Abrego, "Legal Consciousness of Undocumented Latinos."

6 Sara Murray, "Many in U.S. Illegally Overstayed Their Visas," *Wall Street Journal*, April 7, 2013, www.wsj.com; Homeland Security and Governmental Affairs, "Almost Half of Illegal Immigrants Entered U.S. Legally but Stayed after Visa Expired," May 3, 2011, www.hsgac.senate.gov. However, think tanks and nonprofit organizations such as the Pew Hispanic Research Center have also been working to contextualize these trends. For a recent report issued on the topic, see Jeffrey S. Passel and D'Vera Cohn, "Homeland Security Produces First Estimate of Foreign Visitors to U.S. Who Overstay Deadline to Leave," Pew Research Center, February 3, 2015, www.pewresearch.org.

7 Passel and Cohn, "Unauthorized Immigrant Population."

8 Throughout this book, I use the term "Latinx" to refer to individuals hailing from Latin America who are members of the Latinx diaspora. I use this term given its signification of a gender inclusive identity for individuals from this region as it breaks the gender binary often present in the Spanish language to acknowledge the spectrum of sexual identities present among members of this community (www.merriam-webster.com). In spring 2018, the national Latina/o Studies Association, in the call for papers for that year's conference, offered an important analysis of the term, noting, "The 'x' in our conference title graphically denotes acts of resistance and dissent. The 'x' in Latinx questions the traditional binary logic of gender and gendered language, enabling a new dispersion of identity across and beyond 'genders.' At the same time the 'x' invokes a history of alphabetic change to naming and claiming in the Americas" (https://lsa.secure-platform.com). While some may argue that the term "Latinx" is used primarily within the United States and does not fully capture the experiences of Latin American diasporic communities, my use of the term also takes the lead from the activists with whom I worked. Situated within the United States as the location in which they have spent the majority of their adolescence and the context in which their activism has taken place, the undocumented immigrant activists whose experiences I discuss in this book have been significantly influenced by the adoption of this term.

9 García Bedolla, Nakano Glenn, and Escudero, "Working Together to Improve Campus Climate for Undocumented AB540 Students at UC Berkeley."

10 Ngai, *Impossible Subjects*; Romero, "Transnational Chinese Immigrant Smuggling to the United States via Mexico and Cuba."

11 University of California Office of the President, "Annual Report on AB540 Tuition Exemptions 2011–12 Academic Year," June 2013, http://ucop.edu. Also see García Bedolla, Nakano Glenn, and Escudero, "Working Together to Improve Campus Climate for AB540 Undocumented Students at UC Berkeley."

12 For history, see Ngai, *Impossible Subjects*; for sociology, see Menjívar and Kanstroom, *Constructing Immigrant "Illegality"*; for anthropology, see DeGenova, "Migrant 'Illegality' and Deportability in Everyday Life"; Gonzales and Chavez, "'Awakening to a Nightmare'"; Willen, "Toward a Critical Phenomenology of Illegality."

13 Menjívar and Kanstroom, *Constructing Immigrant "Illegality."*

14 DeGenova, "Migrant 'Illegality' and Deportability in Everyday Life," 429.

15 Cacho, *Social Death*.

16 DeGenova and Peutz, *The Deportation Regime*; Menjívar and Kanstroom, *Constructing Immigrant "Illegality."*

17 Gonzales, *Reform without Justice*, Pallares and Flores-González, *Marcha!*; Voss and Bloemraad, *Rallying for Immigrant Rights*; Zepeda-Millán, *Latino Mass Mobilization*.

18 On the family unit, see Dreby, *Everyday Illegal*; Gomberg-Muñoz, *Becoming Legal*; Pallares, *Family Activism*; on labor, see Gleeson, *Precarious Claims*; Gordon, *Suburban Sweatshops*; on religion, see Galvez, *Guadalupe in New York*; Heredia,

"From Prayer to Protest"; on education, see Olivas, *No Undocumented Child Left Behind*; Gonzales, *Lives in Limbo*.

19 In this sense the term "1.5 generation" refers to immigrant youth who were born abroad but entered the United States before adolescence and thus have been socialized similarly to members of the second generation (US-born children of immigrant parents). For further reading on the topic, see Rumbaut, "Generation 1.5, Educational Experiences of."

20 Gleeson and Gonzales, "'When Do Papers Matter?'"; Gonzales, Heredia, and Negrón-Gonzales, "Untangling *Plyler*'s Legacy".

21 Gleeson and Gonzales, "'When Do Papers Matter?'"; McCann, *Rights at Work*.

22 *Plyler v. Doe*, 457 U.S. 202 (1982).

23 Abrego, "'I Can't Go to College Because I Don't Have Papers'"; Gonzales, "Learning to Be Illegal."

24 The Development, Relief, and Education for Alien Minors (DREAM) Act was a bill first introduced in 2001 that, if passed, would have provided qualifying undocumented youth who completed either two years of higher education or service in the US armed forces with a path to US citizenship. In 2006, in response to the Border Protection, Anti-terrorism and Illegal Immigration and Control Act of 2005, which would have, among other things, made assisting an undocumented person a criminal rather than civil charge, mass protests occurred nationally (Pallares and Flores-González, *Marcha!*; Voss and Bloemraad, *Rallying for Immigrant Rights*; Zepeda-Millán, *Latino Mass Mobilization*).

25 Nicholls, *The DREAMers*, 5.

26 Gonzales, "Left Out but Not Shut Down," 232.

27 Chavez, *Queer Migration Politics*; Enriquez and Saguy, "Coming Out of the Shadows"; Villazor, "The Undocumented Closet."

28 Swerts, "Gaining a Voice"; Zimmerman, "Transmedia Testimonio."

29 For an educational context, see Enriquez, "A 'Master Status' or the 'Final Straw'?"; Valdez and Golash-Boza, "Master Status or Intersectional Identity?"; for the intersection of sexuality and immigrant status, see Terriquez, "Intersectional Mobilization, Social Movement Spillover, and Queer Youth Leadership in the Immigrant Rights Movement"; Terriquez, Brenes, and Lopez, "Intersectionality as a Multipurpose Collective Action Frame."

30 Menjívar and Abrego, "Legal Violence."

31 In comparison to anthropologists, law and society scholars have also stressed the need to study "upward." Discussing human rights law in a global context, Merry and colleagues draw upon Santos and Rodriguez-Garavito's "bottom up approach" that "illuminates how law is used by organizations engaged in counterhegemonic activism to contest legal hegemonies, emphasizing the inextricable linkage between law and politics" (Merry et al., "Law from Below," 103).

32 Interviews for the San Francisco Bay Area portion of the study were selected from a larger sample (see Escudero, "Organizing While Undocumented") using a refined search criteria to meet the criteria of this study.

33 Provine et al., *Policing Immigrants*; Villazor, "'Sanctuary Cities' and Local Citizenship."

34 Michael D. Shear and Julie Hirschfeld Davis, "Trump Moves to End DACA and Calls on Congress to Act," *New York Times*, September 5, 2017, https://www.nytimes.com/.

35 National Immigration Law Center, "DACA Litigation Timeline," November 9, 2018, www.nilc.org.

36 The practice of social movement participants seeking rights and recognition from the state to be able to fully take part in democratic political action is representative of what sociologist Mary Bernstein has termed the identity as a goal approach in identity-based social movement activism. Elaborating on this point, Bernstein writes, "Numerous social movements seek acceptance for their identities and these struggles are intertwined with concerns for rights and redistribution," citing examples ranging from French language rights in Quebec to the recognition of communities' indigenous rights in Latin America (Bernstein, "Afterword," 287). This model builds on Bernstein's argument for identity as a goal by examining how groups in some circumstances may not only advocate for recognition of their collective identity as a movement goal but then subsequently seek to exercise those newly won rights. Another example of the need for groups to assert an unrecognized and/or legally denied identity entails the use of identity for organizing purposes in authoritarian regimes (Chen and Moss, "Social Movements and Authoritarian Regimes"; Chua, Mobilizing Gay Singapore; Moss, "Transnational Repression, Diaspora Mobilization, and the Case of the Arab Spring").

37 Polletta and Jasper, "Collective Identity and Social Movements," 285.

38 Polletta and Jasper, 285.

39 Pallares, *Family Activism*. Related to Pallares's discussion of the impossible nature of undocumented immigrant activism, for an analysis of the legal climate in which activists in the immigrant rights movement face, see Gonzales, *Reform without Justice*.

40 Throughout this book I use the term "undocuqueer," acknowledging its development by activists to discuss the experiences of being both undocumented and queer and the unique challenges members of this community face.

CHAPTER 1. THE IDENTITY MOBILIZATION MODEL

1 As discussed in the introduction, the term "undocumented immigrant youth," in this context, refers to as individuals born abroad, but who spent their adolescence in the United States: members of the 1.5 generation. Given that proposed legislation such as the federal DREAM Act and in-state tuition bills defined youth as members of the 1.5 generation from the ages of eighteen to thirty-five today, I use the same definition throughout the text to maintain consistency in terms of the population being discussed.

2 This two-part emphasis dovetails with legal scholar Kimberlé Crenshaw's focus on the structural and political aspects of intersectionality (Crenshaw, "Mapping the Margins").

3   In making the case for an individual and structural analysis of movement activists' use
    of an intersectional collective identity, I draw on theoretical discussions among social
    movement scholars in sociology regarding the importance of examining collective
    identity at the personal and movement-based levels. An analysis of a movement-based
    collective identity is critically informed by the identities of individual movement
    participants. Similarly, I argue that it is necessary to recognize the link between the
    individual and the structural in terms of how activists who emphasize the importance
    of an intersectional movement identity are drawing on the personal in order to eluci-
    date the structural factors needed to understand the marginalization and oppression
    community members face (Whittier, "The Politics of Visibility").

4   Buechler, "New Social Movements and New Social Movement Theory."

5   Blackwell, ¡Chicana Power!; Nishida, "Understanding Political Development
    through an Intersectionality Framework"; Luna, "'Truly a Women of Color
    Organization'"; Ross, "Reproductive Justice as Intersectional Feminist Activism";
    Yuval-Davis, "Intersectionality and Feminist Politics"; Zavella, "Intersectional
    Praxis in the Movement for Reproductive Justice."

6   For an excellent discussion on how collective identity is relevant not only for the
    mobilization of a particular group but also in terms of strategy and a movement's
    overarching goal, see Bernstein, "Celebration and Suppression."

7   Kolenz et al., "Combahee River Collective Statement." For additional histories of
    the concept and its use across the social sciences, see Hancock, Intersectionality; Hill
    Collins and Bilge, Intersectionality; and Hill Collins, "Intersectionality's Definitional
    Dilemmas." While critiques of intersectionality have often pointed to its adoption and
    (mis)use by scholars in other fields, as African American studies and gender and sex-
    uality studies scholar Jennifer Nash has argued, a shift away from the institutionaliza-
    tion of intersectionality and a harkening back to its radical roots can help reclaim the
    potential of an intersectional framework to bring about transformative social change
    for members of oppressed groups (Nash, Black Feminism Reimagined). In a parallel
    fashion, Asad Haider discusses contemporary critiques of identity politics, a concept
    that similarly has a radical tradition but one that has been distorted by its co-optation
    by mainstream and nonradical individuals and movements. Yet, like Nash's argument
    regarding intersectionality, Haider argues that identity politics too can be reclaimed
    and deployed toward a radical, reenvisionist end (Haider, Mistaken Identity).

8   Roberts and Jesudason, "Movement Intersectionality," 314.

9   Roberts and Jesudason, 314–315.

10 For further discussion in the literature on this connection drawing on women-
    of-color feminist scholarship to theorize a process of "coalitional consciousness
    building," see Keating, "Building Coalitional Consciousness."

11 Cohen, "Punks, Bulldaggers and Welfare Queens."

12 Cohen, 461.

13 This notion of a multifaceted, intersectional collective identity framework builds
    on political scientist Lisa García Bedolla's examination of the intersectional nature
    of a collective identity for political engagement (García Bedolla, Fluid Borders)

and sociologist Mary Bernstein's examination of identity for empowerment (Bernstein, "Celebration and Suppression"). In later work Bernstein argues that the concept's development by Verta Taylor and Nancy Whittier can be further expanded upon to "account for the ways movements contend with the realities of individuals' multiple identities [given that an] intersectional approach to identity for empowerment can help explain in more detail how the content of a movement's collective identity is created" (Bernstein, "Afterword," 279).

14 According to sociologists Francesca Polletta and James Jasper, collective identity can be understood as "an individual's cognitive, moral and emotional connection with a broader community, category, practice or institution. It is a perception of a shared status or relation, which may be imagined rather than experienced directly" (Polletta and Jasper, "Collective Identity and Social Movements," 285). While this definition underscores the importance of the individual in the formation of collective identity, scholars have also pointed to the relational aspect with regard to how collective identity is formed as part of a set of negotiations and relationships between individuals holding a shared experience, trait, or characteristic (Fominaya, "Collective Identity in Social Movements").

15 Bernstein, "Afterword," 277–302; Cohen, *The Boundaries of Blackness*.

16 In making the case for a broader examination of collective identity, I draw on sociologist Alberto Melucci's conceptualization of collective identity as an ongoing and continually contested process that movement participants frequently undertake (Fominaya, "Collective Identity in Social Movements").

17 Polletta and Jasper, "Collective Identity and Social Movements," 291–292.

18 In making this argument, I draw on evidence affirming the relevance of multiplicity in terms of movement identities in the LGBTQ movement. In her research, sociologist Elizabeth Armstrong points to the paradox of how the diversification and specialization of movement groups did not lead to fragmentation but instead promoted activism and specialization within the movement (Armstrong, *Forging Gay Identities*).

19 Armstrong, *Forging Gay Identities*; Taylor and Whittier, "Collective Identity in Social Movement Communities."

20 Swidler, "Culture in Action."

21 It is important to note that certain identities are treated in the sociolegal literature as "immutable," namely, the federally protected categories such as race and sex. Yet, as other scholars have pointed out, certain "nonimmutable identities" such as one's religious identity or sexual orientation hold important implications for individuals' everyday lives and constitute an axis on which individuals experience discrimination and marginalization (Clarke, "Against Immutability"). By teasing out the role of the law in working to constitute one's social identity from its related yet distinct use as a tool for organizing and a culturally understood set of values and ideals, the model draws upon Clarke's argument advocating for a more capacious understanding of how these identities operate.

For further discussion of the ways individuals claiming discrimination on the basis of other "nonimmutable categories" must make claims that the marginalization experienced is similar to discrimination on the basis of race and/or sex, see Yoshino, "Assimilation Bias in Equal Protection." For further reading on the role of immigration status as a social identity, see Abrego, "Legitimacy, Social Identity and the Mobilization of Law." Recently, during her keynote address at the Migrant Illegalities across Uneven Legal Geographies Conference at Brown University on October 26, 2018, sociologist Cecilia Menjívar noted that in theorizations of intersectionality and individuals' intersectional lived experiences that take into account one's immigration status, such an identity functions differently than other identities such as race and sex. According to Menjívar, this is because discrimination against individuals due to their legal status is government sanctioned and largely the cumulative result of federal and subfederal laws and policies. With regard to other marginalized identities such as race and sex, federal laws work to protect individuals from discrimination on this basis. Building on Clarke's argument about the need to examine discrimination individuals face due to "immutable" and "nonimmutable" identities, I conceive of an intersectional identity in a manner that considers the multiple levels on which the law and one's legal identity functions.

22 Albiston, "The Dark Side of Litigation as a Social Movement Strategy"; McCann, "Law and Social Movements"; McCann, *Rights at Work*; NeJaime, "Winning through Losing"; Rosenberg, *The Hollow Hope*.

23 Van Dyke and McCammon, *Strategic Alliances*, xiii, xvii–xviii.

24 Freire and Macedo, *The Paulo Freire Reader*; Delgado Bernal et al., *Chicana/Latina Education in Everyday Life*; Cornell, "Las Grenudas"; Sarachild, "Consciousness-Raising"; Whittier, "Identity Politics, Consciousness-Raising and Visibility Politics"; Mansbridge and Morris, *Oppositional Consciousness*.

25 Adam, "Intersectional Coalition"; Carastathis, "Identity Categories as Potential Coalitions"; Chun, Lipsitz, and Shin, "Intersectionality as Social Movement Strategy"; Zavella, "Intersectional Praxis in the Movement for Reproductive Justice."

26 Three notable exceptions to this point are McCammon, *The U.S. Women's Jury Movements and Strategic Adaptation*; Bernstein, "Celebration and Suppression"; and Jasper, "A Strategic Approach to Collective Action."

27 Chavez, *Queer Migration Politics*; Terriquez, "Intersectional Mobilization, Social Movement Spillover, and Queer Youth Leadership in the Immigrant Rights Movement"; and Terriquez, Brenes, and Lopez, "Intersectionality as a Multipurpose Collective Action Frame."

28 McAdam, "Recruitment to High-Risk Activism"; Armbruster-Sandoval, *Starving for Justice*, 3–4.

29 Russo, "Allies Forging a Collective Identity"; Myers, "Ally Identity"; Munkres, "Being Sisters to Salvadoran Peasants."

30 Myers, "Ally Identity," 168.
31 Myers, 172.
32 For further discussion of allyship in the context of social movement activism and additional means of conceptualizing support as a non–directly affected individual, see Tomlinson and Lipsitz, "American Studies as Accompaniment"; Gomberg-Muñoz, "The Complicit Anthropologist."
33 Yoshikawa, *Immigrants Raising Citizens*. Also see Cecilia Menjívar and Andrea Gómez Cervantes, "The Effects of Parental Undocumented Status on Families and Children," American Psychological Association, November 2016, http://www.apa.org.
34 Chun, Lipsitz, and Shin, "Intersectionality as Social Movement Strategy."
35 Bernstein and Olsen, "Identity Deployment and Social Change," 872.
36 Bernstein, "Celebration and Suppression."
37 Carastathis, "Identity Categories as Potential Coalitions."
38 Hancock, *Intersectionality*; Hill Collins and Bilge, *Intersectionality*.
39 Gamson, "Must Identity Movements Self-Destruct?," 401.
40 Gamson, 403.
41 Pallares, *Family Activism*.
42 Nash, *Black Feminism Reimagined*. On "migrant illegality," see Menjívar and Kanstroom, *Constructing Immigrant "Illegality."*
43 Marcus, "Ethnography in/of the World System."
44 Fitzgerald, "Towards a Theoretical Ethnography of Migration."
45 Gonzales, *Lives in Limbo*; Nicholls, *The DREAMers*.
46 For Chicago, see Pallares and Flores-González, *Marcha!*; for Boston, see Cebulko, *Documented, Undocumented and Something Else*.
47 Nicholls and Uitermark, *Cities and Social Movements*, 9.
48 "Largest Cities by U.S. Population," Ballotopedia, December 21, 2018, https://ballotpedia.org.
49 City and County of San Francisco Office of the Mayor, "We Are a Sanctuary City," January 10, 2019, https://sfmayor.org; City of Chicago Office of the Mayor, "Sanctuary City Supportive Resources," January 10, 2019, www.chicago.gov; and "DeBlasio Administration Announces Citywide Guidance and NYPD Protocol to Codify Restrictions on Assistance with Federal Immigration Enforcement," the Official Website of the City of New York, January 10, 2019, www1.nyc.gov.
50 For instance, see the IDNYC website and program at https://access.nyc.gov.
51 Gleeson and Gonzales, "'When Do Papers Matter?'"
52 Holston, *Cities and Citizenship*; Sassen, "The Global City"; Nicholls and Uitermark, *Citizens and Social Movements*, 8.
53 Bernstein, "Identity Politics"; Polletta and Jasper, "Collective Identity and Social Movements"; Reger, Myers, and Einwohner, *Identity Work in Social Movements*; Stryker, Owens, and White, *Self, Identity, and Social Movements*.
54 Kurtz, *Workplace Justice*; Moon, "Who Am I and Who Are We?"
55 For instance, see Chavez, *The Latino Threat Narrative*.

56 Lee, *At America's Gates.*

57 Golash-Boza, "The Immigration Industrial Complex," 296.

58 Ngai, *Impossible Subjects.*

59 Romero, "Transnational Chinese Immigrant Smuggling to the United States via Mexico and Cuba."

60 Ngai, *Impossible Subjects.*

61 Wu, *The Model Minority Myth,* 2.

62 Passel and Cohn, "Unauthorized Immigrant Population"; Buenavista and Tran, "Undocumented Immigrant Students."

63 Buenavista, "Model (Undocumented) Minorities and 'Illegal' Immigrants"; Buenavista and Chen, "Intersections and Crossroads"; Cho, "A Double Bind"; Dao, "Out and Asian." See also Momo Chang, "Dreams Deferred," *Hyphen: Asian America Unabridged,* May 15, 2012, https://hyphenmagazine.com. Another example is Tom Wong's white paper detailing the importance of collecting additional data to supplement the experiences of Asian American Pacific Islander (AAPI) undocumented immigrant community members (Tom K. Wong, "Reaching Undocumented Asian Americans and Pacific Islanders in the United States," Center for Migration Studies, http://cmsny.org).

64 On the experiences of South Asian immigrant youth, see Maira, *Missing.*

65 Wong et al., *Undocumented and Unafraid.*

66 Amanda Holpuch, "Undocumented, Asian, and Taking Up Arms in the Immigration Fight—Finally," *Guardian,* August 23, 2015, www.theguardian.com; NAKASEC, "Launch of the National AAPI DACA Video Tour," April 12, 2016, http://nakasec.org.

67 Cisneros and Bracho, "Coming Out of the Shadows and the Closet"; Cisneros, "Working with the Complexity and Refusing to Simplify"; Chavez, *Queer Migration Politics*; Terriquez, "Intersectional Mobilization, Social Movement Spillover, and Queer Youth Leadership in the Immigrant Rights Movement"; Lubhéid, *Entry Denied*; Lubhéid and Cantú, *Queer Migrations.*

68 See I. E. Vasquez, "Our Stories—Our Power," YouTube, January 18, 2012, www.youtube.com/watch?v=J_2Dzy81k0A.

69 See Brave New Foundation, "Undocumented and Unafraid; Queer and Unashamed," YouTube, February 13, 2012, www.youtube.com/watch?v=kIi3cPArnDU&list=PLpcK6aelw4n2D5E3CldFD1paq2BK5P-Qt.

70 See Carlos Padilla, "Undocumented. Unafraid. Queer. Unashamed," *HuffPost,* February 12, 2015, www.huffingtonpost.com.

71 Seif, "'Coming Out of the Shadows' and 'Undocuqueer'"; Enriquez and Saguy, "Coming Out of the Shadows."

72 Tomchin, "Bodies and Bureaucracy"; Villazor, "The Undocumented Closet." In this article Villazor discusses the intersection of queer individuals' efforts to codify a right to marriage and the limited opportunities for undocumented immigrants to adjust their status through marriage to a US citizen. Until 2004, following the Supreme Court's striking down of the federal Defense of

Marriage Act (DOMA), same-sex and transgender-identified undocumented spouses of US citizens were eligible for fiancé visas. The shift that took place in 2004 with the end of DOMA thus had a key impact on the lives of undocuqueer community members through the cultivation of this group's legal and social consciousness had just begun. For further discussion of the complex, interrelated histories of family law and immigration law, see Figueroa, "'The Slow, Yet Long-Anticipated Death of DOMA and Its Impact on Immigration Law"; Shah, "LGBT Identity in Immigration." See also Immigration Equality, "Family. Unvalued: Discrimination, Denial, and the Fate of Binational Same-Sex Couples under U.S. Law," 2006, www.hrw.org.

73 Chavez, *Queer Migration Politics*, 4.

74 Hondagneu-Sotelo, "New Directions in Gender and Immigration Research"; Hondagneu-Sotelo, *Gender and U.S. Immigration*; Hondagneu-Sotelo, *Domestica*; Hondagneu-Sotelo, *Gendered Transitions*.

75 On women's decision to leave their home countries, see Donato, "U.S. Migration from Latin America"; Donato et al., "A Glass Half Full?"; Hondagneu-Sotelo, *Gendered Transitions*; on transnational parenting and caring practices, see Abrego, *Sacrificing Families*; Hondagneu-Sotelo and Avila, "'I'm Here, but I'm There"; Parreñas, "Transnational Mothering"; on violence targeting immigrant mothers and women, see Abrego and Menjívar, "Immigrant Latina Mothers as Targets of Legal Violence"; Romero, "Constructing Mexican Immigrant Women as a Threat to American Families"; on the gendered nature of the US naturalization process, see Salcido and Menjívar, "Gendered Paths to Legal Citizenship."

76 On undocumented immigrant men, see Das Gupta, "'Don't Deport Our Daddies'"; Golash-Boza and Hondagneu-Sotelo, "Latino Immigrant Men and the Deportation Crisis"; on queer immigrant men, see Carrillo, *Pathways of Desire*; Roque Ramirez, "Claiming Queer Cultural Citizenship."

77 Leon, "Marriage and Legalization"; Enriquez, "Gendering Illegality"; Pila, "'I'm Not Good Enough for Anyone'"; López, "'Impossible Families.'"

78 Donato, Enriquez, and Llewellyn, "Frozen and Stalled?"

79 Gomberg-Muñoz, *Becoming Legal*.

80 Gomberg-Muñoz, 11.

81 Gomberg-Muñoz, 12.

82 Leon, "Marriage and Legalization," 29.

83 Leon, 32, 42.

CHAPTER 2. ASIAN AND UNDOCUMENTED

1 "IJYL Out of the Shadows 2011," YouTube, April 2, 2011, www.youtube.com/watch?v=bATPoDrxkAA. Although Karla was not an interviewee for this project, I draw on her speech to highlight a broader trend among participants in my research study: the importance of cultivating a political consciousness among Asian undocumented immigrant youth.

2 Lee, *At America's Gates*; Ngai, *Impossible Subjects*.

3 Ancheta, *Race, Rights, and the Asian American Experience*; Baldoz, *The Third Asiatic Migration*.

4 Romero, "Transnational Chinese Immigrant Smuggling to the United States via Mexico and Cuba"; Ngai, *Impossible Subjects*.

5 Romero, "Transnational Chinese Immigrant Smuggling to the United States via Mexico and Cuba"; Ngai, *Impossible Subjects*.

6 Molina, *How Race Is Made in America*, 6–7.

7 Chou and Feagin, *The Myth of the Model Minority*.

8 Polletta, *It Was Like a Fever*, 3.

9 Polletta, 3.

10 Ewick and Silbey, *The Common Place of Law*.

11 For further discussion of storytelling in social movements and the art of crafting one's story, see Polletta, *It Was Like a Fever*; Polletta et al., "The Sociology of Storytelling." Also see Tilly and Tarrow, *Contentious Politics*; Tilly, *Regimes and Repertoires*.

12 García Bedolla, Nakano Glenn, and Escudero, "Working Together to Improve Campus Climate for Undocumented AB540 Students at UC Berkeley."

13 García Bedolla, Nakano Glenn, and Escudero. AB540 is a California bill, passed in 2001, that provides access to paying in-state tuition for graduates of a California high school. For more information, see "AB 540 Nonresident Tuition Exemption," University of California, http://admission.universityofcalifornia.edu.

14 García Bedolla, Nakano Glenn, and Escudero, "Working Together to Improve Campus Climate for Undocumented AB540 Students at UC Berkeley."

15 Gomberg-Muñoz, *Labor and Legality*.

16 Steven Radelet and Jeffrey Sachs, "The Onset of the Asian Financial Crisis" (Cambridge, MA: National Bureau of Economic Research), www.nber.org.

17 Chou and Feagin, *The Myth of the Model Minority*.

18 Patler, "Racialized Illegality."

19 For more information about the graphic novel Undocumented: The Architecture of Migrant Detention, discussed at the event, see the book's website: http://undocumented.ca.

20 For more information about the event and its purpose, see "Undocumented Architecture," Asian American Writers' Workshop, http://aaww.org.

21 RAISE and DRUM are two New York City–based, Asian undocumented youth organizations that have collaborated with the AAWW to hold community events and gatherings. More information can be found at http://aaldef.org and www.drumnyc.org, respectively.

22 More information about the zine, *Amplify(HER)*, and selections from the zine itself, can be found on the Asian American Writer's Workshop website: http://aaww.org.

23 One Eyelash, "A Cause Worth Fighting For," in *Amplify(HER)*.

24 Gonzales, "Learning to Be Illegal."

25 Nicholls, *The DREAMers*.

26 See the special issue on immigrant deservingness and the politics of respectability coedited by Genevieve Negrón-Gonzales, Leisy Abrego, and Kathleen Coll
entitled "Complicating the Politics of Deservingness: A Critical Look at Latina/o
Migrant Youth." The special issue was published in 2015 in the *Association of
Mexican American Educators Journal*: http://amaejournal.utsa.edu.

27 Comments from Azucena come from García Bedolla, Nakano Glenn, and Escudero, "Working Together to Improve Campus Climate for Undocumented AB540
Students at UC Berkeley." In a previous article the author incorrectly referred to
Azucena as a student at a California State University campus. She was in fact a
student at another large public university in the San Francisco Bay Area (Escudero, "Organizing While Undocumented"). The DREAMer identity emerged in
2001 following Senators Dick Durbin and Orin Hatch's initial introduction of the
DREAM Act. This act, if passed, would have provided a subset of undocumented
immigrant youth—those pursuing a college degree and/or those serving in the US
armed forces—with a path to citizenship (Nicholls, *The DREAMers*). However, as
activists and academics alike have shown, a DREAMer lens has grave limitations,
portraying a subgroup of undocumented immigrants as more worthy and deserv-
ing of citizenship than others (Pallares, *Family Activism*; Chauvin and Garcés-
Mascareñas, "Becoming Less Illegal."

28 García Bedolla, Nakano Glenn, and Escudero, "Working Together to Improve
Campus Climate for Undocumented AB540 Students at UC Berkeley."

29 The individual whose responses are referenced using the pseudonym Kamol
in this manuscript was referred to using the pseudonym Steven in the earlier
research report by García Bedolla, Nakano Glenn, and Escudero, "Working
Together to Improve Campus Climate for Undocumented AB540 Students at UC
Berkeley").

30 García Bedolla, Nakano Glenn, and Escudero.

31 Pulido, *Black, Brown, Yellow, and Left*.

32 For further discussion of how anti-Latinx sentiment has developed over time,
particularly against Mexican immigrants, who constitute the largest proportion
of undocumented immigrants in the United States today, see Chavez, *The Latino
Threat Narrative*.

33 Perez Huber et al., "Getting beyond the 'Symptom.'"

CHAPTER 3. UNDOCUQUEER ACTIVISM

1 Raquel Reichard, "Why This Undocumented Latina Launched Coming Out of the
Shadows Month," *Latina*, March 7, 2016, www.latina.com.

2 Throughout this chapter, I use multiple terms to refer to the experiences of
gay and lesbian individuals, including "queer" and "LGBTQ." I recognize the
unique histories of each term, in particular the reappropriation of "queer" as
an empowering term. Others, however, have critiqued "queer" as an identity
category as it furthers a centering of heteronormativity as "the norm" and

homosexuality as difference (Lillian Rivera, "Am I Queer? Nope. Just Familia Please," *HuffPost*, August 21, 2016, www.huffingtonpost.com). Rather than seeking to make a statement on which term is appropriate and/or more accurate, I utilize the terminology that the individuals with whom I spoke drew upon in our conversations.

3 Tilly and Tarrow, *Contentious Politics*; Della Porta, "Repertoires of Contention."

4 Terriquez, "Intersectional Mobilization, Social Movement Spillover, and Queer Youth Leadership in the Immigrant Rights Movement."

5 For a discussion of the coconstitutive nature of sexual orientation and immigrant identity, see Epstein and Carrillo, "Immigrant Sexual Citizenship."

6 Canaday, *The Straight State*.

7 Queer of color critique can be seen in the work of scholars such as José Estéban Muñoz, Roderick Ferguson, Jafari Allen, and Grace Hong.

8 Gould, *Moving Politics*, 19.

9 Gould, 19–20.

10 Immigrant Youth Justice League, "National Coming Out of the Shadows Month 2013," www.iyjl.org, accessed on January 4, 2019.

11 Immigrant Youth Justice League.

12 Immigrant Youth Justice League, "Coming Out: Undocumented, Unafraid, Unapologetic," YouTube, www.youtube.com/watch?v=jPNlpzykojE, accessed on January 4, 2019.

13 Immigrant Youth Justice League, "IYJL Out of the Shadows 2011," YouTube, www.youtube.com/watch?v=bATPoDrxkAA, accessed on January 4, 2019.

14 Gleeson and Gonzales, "'When Do Papers Matter?'"

15 Burke and Bernstein, "How the Right Usurped the Queer Agenda"; Hull, *Same-Sex Marriage*; Leachman, "From Protest to *Perry*."

16 Human Rights Campaign, "HRC Story," www.hrc.org, accessed on January 4, 2019.

17 Hondagneu-Sotelo, *Religion and Social Justice for Immigrants*.

18 Prerna Lal, "How Queer Undocumented Youth Built the Immigrant Rights Movement," *HuffPost*, March 28, 213, www.huffingtonpost.com.

19 David Agren, "Migrant Caravan: Weary, Frustrated Participants Face a Long, Dangerous Road Ahead," *USA Today*, November 4, 2018, www.usatoday.com.

20 "Caravan at Mexico-Guatemala Border Shrinks as Migrants Cross," PBS News Hour, October 20, 2018, www.pbs.org.

21 "What It's Like to Be Queer and Undocumented," YouTube, June 7, 2018, www.youtube.com/watch?v=CfwDflt9aLQ&feature=youtube.

CHAPTER 4. FORMERLY UNDOCUMENTED ACTIVISTS

1 Menjívar and Morando, "Transformative Effects of Immigration Law," 1834.

2 Pérez Huber, "Healing Images and Narratives"; Pérez Huber, "Using Latina/o Critical Race Theory (LatCrit) and Racist Nativism to Explore Intersectionality in the Educational Experiences of Undocumented Chicana College Students"; Mu-

ñoz and Maldonado, "Counterstories of College Persistence by Undocumented Mexicana Students."

3 *Plyler v. Doe*, 457 U.S. 202 (1982).

4 For further reading on the topic, see Pallares, *Family Activism*. Moreover, boundary making is a rich theoretical field within the sociological literature that discusses the means by which boundaries are created and negotiated. I argue that this literature can potentially have resonance in the context of the immigrant rights movement regarding this discussion of centering the experiences of "directly affected individuals." For additional reading on boundary making's connection to the construction of a collective identity, see Lamont and Molnár, "The Study of Boundaries in the Social Sciences."

5 Abrams, "Emotions in the Mobilization of Rights," 581.

6 Nicholls, *The DREAMers*.

7 Gonzales, "Learning to Be Illegal."

8 Nakano Glenn, *Forced to Care*, 5.

9 García Bedolla, Nakano Glenn, and Escudero, "Working Together to Improve Campus Climate for Undocumented AB540 Students at UC Berkeley."

10 A Chicana and/or Chicano identity is primarily understood as referring to the experiences of Mexican American community members residing in the US Southwest. Some have also discussed Chicano identity, or its theorization of Chicanismo, as a political ideology outlined in founding documents of the student organization Movimiento Estudiantil Chicana and Chicano de Aztlán (MEChA). For further readings on Chicana identity, Chicanismo, and the Chicano movement, see Blackwell, *¡Chicana Power!*; García, *Chicanismo*; and Montejano, *Quixote's Soldiers*.

11 Social movement scholars have extensively examined the critical role of emotions in activism. For more information on this subset of the social movement literature, see Goodwin, Jasper, and Polletta, *Passionate Politics*.

12 Gonzales, *Lives in Limbo*.

13 Muzaffar Chishti, "Senate Blocks Passage of DREAM Act by Five Votes," Migration Policy Institute, December 21, 2010, www.migrationpolicy.org.

CONCLUSION

1 As George M. Maney and colleagues note, a focus on strategy points to an area in which social movement theory and scholarship can become of interest to movement activists and participants. They write, "Activists typically find little insight from academic theory and research on social movements. Yet strategy provides an important point of convergence where the theoretical and methodological tools of the discipline can be harnessed around questions of ongoing significance for practitioners" (Maney et al., "An Introduction to Strategies for Social Change," 17).

2 Armenta, *Protect, Serve, and Deport*; Menjívar and Kanstroom, *Constructing Immigrant "Illegality."*

3   Armenta, *Protect, Serve, and Deport*; García, *Legal Passing.*

4   Black Alliance for Just Immigration, "Who We Are," http://baji.org.

5   Waters, *Black Identities.*

6   Orie Givens, "Obama Disrupter Jennicet Gutierrez: Still Resisting," *Advocate*, June
    10, 2016, www.advocate.com.

7   For an in-depth description of the organization, its campaigns, and issues around
    which its members organize, see Familia: Trans Queer Liberation Movement,
    http://familiatqlm.org.

8   Not One More, "White House Pride Event Interrupted over LGBTQ Detention,"
    YouTube, June 24, 2015, www.youtube.com/watch?v=vv9wRNuptC8.

9   Puar, *Terrorist Assemblages.*

10 Lisa Fernandez, "Ju Hong, UC Berkeley Graduate, Heckles President Obama on
    Deportation," NBC Bay Area, November 25, 2013, www.nbcbayarea.com; "Presi-
    dent Obama, Stop Separating and Deporting Our Families," *HuffPost*, December
    2, 2013, www.huffingtonpost.com.

11 Katie Reilly, "Here's What President Trump Has Said about DACA in the Past,"
    Time, September 5, 2017, http:///time.com.

12 Tal Kopanoi:, "Trump Ends DACA but Gives Congress Window to Save It," CNN,
    September 5, 2017, www.cnn.com.

13 "Supreme Court Allows Trump Travel Ban to Take Effect," *New York Times,* De-
    cember 4, 2017, www.nytimes.com.

APPENDIX B. METHODOLOGICAL NOTES

1   Mendez, "Globalizing Scholar Activism," 139.

2   Hale, *Engaging Contradictions*, xxii.

3   Menjívar and Kanstroom, *Constructing Immigrant "Illegality"*; Ruszczyk and Bar-
    bosa, "A Second Generation of Immigrant Illegality Studies."

4   Delgado Bernal and Villalpando, "An Apartheid of Knowledge in Academia."

BIBLIOGRAPHY

Abrams, Kathryn. "Emotions in the Mobilization of Rights." *Harvard Civil Rights–Civil Liberties Law Review* 46 (2011): 551–589.

Abrego, Leisy. "'I Can't Go to College Because I Don't Have Papers': Incorporation Patterns of Latino Undocumented Youth." *Latino Studies* 4, no. 3 (2006): 212–231.

———. "Legal Consciousness of Undocumented Latinos: Fear and Stigma as Barriers to Claims-Making for First- and 1.5-Generation Immigrants." *Law and Society Review* 45 no. 2 (2011): 337–370.

———. "Legitimacy, Social Identity and the Mobilization of Law: The Effects of Assembly Bill 540 on Undocumented Students in California." *Law and Social Inquiry* 33, no. 3 (2008): 709–734.

———. *Sacrificing Families: Navigating Laws, Labor and Love across Borders.* Stanford, CA: Stanford University Press, 2014.

Abrego, Leisy J., and Cecilia Menjívar. "Immigrant Latina Mothers as Targets of Legal Violence." *International Journal of Sociology of the Family* 37, no. 1 (2011): 9–26.

Adam, Erin. "Intersectional Coalition: The Paradoxes of Rights-Based Movement Building in LGBTQ and Immigrant Communities." *Law and Society Review* 51, no. 1 (2017): 132–167.

Albiston, Catherine. "The Dark Side of Litigation as a Social Movement Strategy." *Iowa Law Review Bulletin* 96 (2011): 61–77.

Ancheta, Angelo. *Race, Rights, and the Asian American Experience.* New Brunswick, NJ: Rutgers University Press, 1998.

Armbruster-Sandoval, Ralph. *Starving for Justice: Hunger Strikes, Spectacular Speech, and the Struggle for Dignity.* Tucson: University of Arizona Press, 2017.

Armenta, Amada. *Protect, Serve, and Deport: The Rise of Policing as Immigration Enforcement.* Berkeley: University of California Press, 2017.

Armstrong, Elizabeth. *Forging Gay Identities: Organizing Sexuality in San Francisco, 1950–1994.* Chicago: University of Chicago Press, 2002.

Baldoz, Rick. *The Third Asiatic Migration: Migration and Empire in Filipino America, 1898–1946.* New York: New York University Press.

Bernstein, Mary. "Afterword: The Analytic Dimensions of Identity: A Political Identity Framework." In *Identity Work in Social Movements,* edited by Jo Reger, Daniel J. Myers, and Rachel L. Einwohner, 277–302. Minneapolis: University of Minnesota Press, 2008.

———. "Celebration and Suppression: The Strategic Uses of Identity by the Lesbian and Gay Movement." *American Journal of Sociology* 103, no. 3 (1997): 531–565.

————. "Identity Politics." *Annual Review of Sociology* 31 (2005): 47–74.

Bernstein, Mary, and Kristine A. Olsen. "Identity Deployment and Social Change: Understanding Identity as a Social Movement and Organizing Strategy." *Sociology Compass* 3, no. 6 (2009): 871–883.

Blackwell, Maylei. *¡Chicana Power! Contested Histories of Feminism in the Chicano Movement.* Austin: University of Texas Press, 2011.

Buechler, Steven M. "New Social Movements and New Social Movement Theory." In *The Wiley-Blackwell Encyclopedia of Social and Political Movements*, edited by David A. Snow, Donatella della Porta, Bert Klandermans, and Doug McAdam. Malden, MA: Wiley, 2013.

Buenavista, Tracy. "Model (Undocumented) Minorities and 'Illegal' Immigrants: Centering Asian Americans and US Carcerality in Undocumented Student Discourse." *Race, Ethnicity and Education* 21, no. 1 (2018): 78–91.

Buenavista, Tracy, and Angela Chuan-Ru Chen. "Intersections and Crossroads: A Counter-story of an Undocumented Asian American College Student." In *The Misrepresented Minority: New Insights on Asian Americans and Pacific Islanders, and the Implications for Higher Education*, edited by Samuel D. Museus, Dina C. Maramba, and Robert T. Teranishi, 198–212. Sterling, VA: Stylus Publishing, 2013.

Buenavista, Tracy, and Tam Tran. "Undocumented Immigrant Students." In *Encyclopedia of Asian American Issues Today*, edited by Grace J. Yoo and Edith Wen-Chu Chen, 253–257. Westport, CT: Greenwood Press, 2010.

Burke, Mary C., and Mary Bernstein. "How the Right Usurped the Queer Agenda: Frame Co-optation in Political Discourse." *Sociological Forum* 29, no. 4 (2014): 830–850.

Cacho, Lisa Marie. *Social Death: Racialized Rightlessness and the Criminalization of the Unprotected.* New York: New York University Press, 2012.

Canaday, Margot. *The Straight State: Sexuality and Citizenship in Twentieth-Century America.* Princeton, NJ: Princeton University Press, 2011.

Carastathis, Anna. "Identity Categories as Potential Coalitions." *Signs* 38, no. 4 (2013): 941–965.

Carrillo, Héctor. *Pathways of Desire: The Sexual Migration of Mexican Gay Men.* Durham, NC: Duke University Press, 2017.

Cebulko, Kara. *Documented, Undocumented and Something Else: The Incorporation of Children of Brazilian Immigrants.* El Paso, TX: LFB Scholarly Press, 2013.

Chauvin, Sébastian, and Blanca Garcés-Mascareñas. "Becoming Less Illegal: Deservingness Frames and Undocumented Migrant Incorporation." *Sociology Compass* 8 (2014): 422–432.

Chavez, Karma. *Queer Migration Politics: Activist Rhetoric and Coalitional Possibilities.* Urbana: University of Illinois Press, 2013.

Chavez, Leo. *The Latino Threat Narrative: Constructing Immigrants, Citizens and the Nation.* Stanford, CA: Stanford University Press, 2008.

Chen, Xi, and Dana Moss. "Social Movements and Authoritarian Regimes." In *The Blackwell Companion to Social Movements*, edited by David Snow, Sarah Soule, Hanspeter Kriesi, and Holly McCammon, 666–681. Malden, MA: Blackwell, 2018.

Cho, Esther Yoona. "A Double Bind: 'Model Minority' and 'Illegal Alien.'" *Asian American Law Journal* 24 (2017): 123–130.

Chou, Rosalind S., and Joe R. Feagin. *The Myth of the Model Minority*. New York: Routledge, 2016.

Chua, Lynette. *Mobilizing Gay Singapore: Rights and Resistance in the Authoritarian State*. Philadelphia: Temple University Press, 2014.

Chun, Jennifer Jihye, George Lipsitz, and Young Shin. "Intersectionality as Social Movement Strategy: Asian Immigrant Women Advocates." *Signs* 38, no. 4 (2013): 917–940.

Cisneros, Jesus. "Working with the Complexity and Refusing to Simplify: Undocuqueer Meaning Making at the Intersection of LGBTQ and Immigrant Rights Discourses." *Journal of Homosexuality* 64, no. 13 (2017): 1415–1434.

Cisneros, Jesus, and Christian Bracho. "Coming Out of the Shadows and the Closet: Visibility Schemas among Undocuqueer Immigrants." *Journal of Homosexuality* 65, no. 9 (2018): 1–20.

Clarke, Jessica A. "Against Immutability." *Yale Law Journal* 125, no. 1 (2015): 1–325.

Cohen, Cathy. *The Boundaries of Blackness: AIDS and the Breakdown of Black Politics*. Chicago: University of Chicago Press, 1999.

———. "Punks, Bulldaggers and Welfare Queens: The Radical Potential of Queer Politics?" *GLQ: A Journal of Lesbian and Gay Studies* 3, no. 4 (1997): 437–465.

Cornell, Drucilla. "Las Grenudas: Recollections on Consciousness-Raising." *Signs* 25, no. 4 (2000): 1033–1039.

Crenshaw, Kimberlé. "Mapping the Margins: Intersectionality, Identity Politics, and Violence against Women of Color." *Stanford Law Review* 43, no. 6 (1991): 1241–1299.

Dao, Loan. "Out and Asian: How Undocu/DACAmented Asian Americans and Pacific Islander Youth Navigate Dual Liminality in the Immigrant Rights Movement." *Societies* 7, no. 3 (2017): 1–15.

Das Gupta, Monisha. "'Don't Deport Our Daddies': Gendering State Deportation Practices and Immigrant Organizing." *Gender and Society* 28, no. 1 (2014): 83–109.

DeGenova, Nicholas P. "Migrant 'Illegality' and Deportability in Everyday Life." *Annual Review of Anthropology* 31 (2002): 419–447.

DeGenova, Nicholas P., and Nathalie Peutz, eds. *The Deportation Regime: Sovereignty, Space and the Freedom of Movement*. Durham, NC: Duke University Press, 2010.

Delgado Bernal, Dolores, C. Alejandra Elenes, Francisca E. Godinez, and Sofia Villenas, eds. *Chicana/Latina Education in Everyday Life: Feminista Perspectives on Pedagogy and Epistemology*. Albany: State University of New York Press, 2006.

Delgado Bernal, Dolores, and Octavio Villalpando. "An Apartheid of Knowledge in Academia: The Struggle over the 'Legitimate' Knowledge of Faculty of Color." *Equity and Excellence in Education* 35, no. 2 (2010): 169–180.

Della Porta, Donatella. "Repertoires of Contention." In *The Wiley-Blackwell Encyclopedia of Social and Political Movements*, edited by David Snow, Donatella Della Porta, Bret Klandermans, and Doug McAdam. Hoboken, NJ: Wiley, 2014.

Donato, Katharine. "U.S. Migration from Latin America: Gendered Shifts and Patterns." *Annals of the American Academy* 630, no. 1 (2010): 78–92.

Donato, Katharine, Laura Enriquez, and Cheryl Llewellyn. "Frozen and Stalled? Gender and Migration Scholarship in the 21st Century." *American Behavioral Scientist* 61, no. 10 (2017): 1079–1085.

Donato, Katharine M., Donna Gabaccia, Jennifer Holdaway, Martin Manalansan IV, and Patricia R. Pessar. "A Glass Half Full? Gender in Migration Studies." *International Migration Review* 40, no. 1 (2006): 3–26.

Dreby, Joanna. *Everyday Illegal: When Policies Undermine Immigrant Families*. Berkeley: University of California Press, 2015.

Enriquez, Laura. "Gendering Illegality: Undocumented Young Adults' Negotiation of the Family Formation Process." *American Behavioral Scientist* 61, no. 10 (2017): 1153–1171.

———. "A 'Master Status' or the 'Final Straw'? Assessing the Role of Immigration Status in Latino Undocumented Young Adults' Pathways Out of School." *Journal of Ethnic and Migration Studies* 43, no. 9 (2017): 1526–1543.

Enriquez, Laura, and Abigail Saguy. "Coming Out of the Shadows: Harnessing a Cultural Schema to Advance the Undocumented Immigrant Movement." *American Journal of Cultural Sociology* 4, no. 1 (2015): 107–130.

Epstein, Steve, and Héctor Carrillo. "Immigrant Sexual Citizenship: Intersectional Templates among Mexican Gay Immigrants to the United States." *Citizenship Studies* 18, nos. 3–4 (2014): 259–276.

Escudero, Kevin. "Organizing While Undocumented: The Law as a 'Double Edged Sword' in the Movement to Pass the DREAM Act." *the crit* 6, no. 2 (2013): 31–52.

Ewick, Patricia, and Susan Silbey. *The Common Place of Law: Stories from Everyday Life*. Chicago: University of Chicago Press, 1998.

Figueroa, Laura. "'The Slow, Yet Long-Anticipated Death of DOMA and Its Impact on Immigration Law: Where Are We Two Years Later?" *St. Mary's Law Review on Race and Social Justice* 16, no. 3 (2014): 547–584.

Fitzgerald, David. "Towards a Theoretical Ethnography of Migration." *Qualitative Sociology* (2006). doi:10.1007/s11133-005-9005-6.

Fominaya, Cristina Flesher. "Collective Identity in Social Movements: Central Concepts and Debates." *Sociology Compass* 4, no. 6 (2010): 393–404.

Freire, Ana Maria Aaraújo, and Donaldo Macedo. *The Paulo Freire Reader*. New York: Continuum, 1998.

Galvez, Alyshia. *Guadalupe in New York: Devotion and the Struggle for Citizenship Rights among Mexican Immigrants*. New York: New York University Press, 2009.

Gamson, Joshua. "Must Identity Movements Self-Destruct? A Queer Dilemma." *Social Problems* 42, no. 3 (1995): 390–407.

García, Angela. *Legal Passing: Navigating Undocumented Life and Local Immigration Law*. Berkeley: University of California Press, 2019.

García, Ignacio M. *Chicanismo: The Forging of a Militant Ethos among Mexican Americans*. Tucson: University of Arizona Press, 1997.

García Bedolla, Lisa. *Fluid Borders: Latino Power, Identity and Politics in Los Angeles.* Berkeley: University of California Press, 2005.

García Bedolla, Lisa, Evelyn Nakano Glenn, and Kevin Escudero. "Working Together to Improve Campus Climate for Undocumented AB540 Students at UC Berkeley." Berkeley, CA: UC Berkeley Center for Race and Gender and Center for Latino Policy Research, February 2013. www.crg.berkeley.edu.

Gleeson, Shannon. *Precarious Claims: The Promise and Failure of Workplace Protections in the United States.* Berkeley: University of California Press, 2016.

Gleeson, Shannon, and Roberto G. Gonzales. "'When Do Papers Matter?' An Institutional Analysis of Undocumented Life in the United States." *International Migration Review* 50, no. 4 (2012): 1–19.

Golash-Boza, Tanya. "The Immigration Industrial Complex: Why We Enforce Immigration Policies Destined to Fail." *Sociology Compass* 3, no. 2 (2009): 295–309.

Golash-Boza, Tanya, and Pierette Hondagneu-Sotelo. "Latino Immigrant Men and the Deportation Crisis: A Gendered Racial Removal Program." *Latino Studies* 11, no. 3 (2013): 271–292.

Gomberg-Muñoz, Ruth. "The Complicit Anthropologist." *Journal for the Anthropology of North America* 21, no. 1 (2018): 36–37.

———. *Becoming Legal: Immigration Law and Mixed-Status Families.* New York: Oxford University Press, 2016.

———. *Labor and Legality: An Ethnography of a Mexican Immigrant Network.* New York: Oxford University Press, 2011.

Gonzales, Alfonso. *Reform without Justice: Latino Migrant Politics and the Homeland Security State.* New York: Oxford University Press, 2013.

Gonzales, Roberto G. "Learning to Be Illegal: Undocumented Youth and Shifting Legal Contexts in the Transition to Adulthood." *American Sociological Review* 76, no. 4 (2011): 602–619.

———. "Left Out but Not Shut Down: Political Activism and the Undocumented Student Movement." *Northwestern Journal of Law and Social Policy* 3 (2008): 219–239.

———. *Lives in Limbo: Undocumented and Coming of Age in America.* Berkeley: University of California Press, 2015.

Gonzales, Roberto G., and Leo R. Chavez. "'Awakening to a Nightmare': Abjectivity and Illegality in the Lives of 1.5-Generation Latino Immigrants in the United States." *Current Anthropology* 53, no. 3 (2012): 255–281.

Gonzales, Roberto G., Luisa L. Heredia, and Genevieve Negrón-Gonzales. "Untangling Plyler's Legacy." *Harvard Educational Review* 85 (2015): 318–341.

Goodwin, Jeff, James Jasper, and Francesca Polletta, eds. *Passionate Politics: Emotions and Social Movements.* Chicago: University of Chicago Press, 2001.

Gordon, Jennifer. *Suburban Sweatshops: The Fight for Immigrant Rights.* Cambridge, MA: Harvard University Press, 2007.

Gould, Deborah B. *Moving Politics: Emotion and Act Up's Fight against AIDS.* Chicago: University of Chicago Press, 2009.

Haider, Asad. *Mistaken Identity.* Brooklyn: Verso, 2018.

Hale, Charles R., ed. *Engaging Contradictions: Theory, Politics and Methods of Activist Scholarship.* Berkeley: University of California Press, 2008.

Hancock, Ange-Marie. *Intersectionality: An Intellectual History.* New York: Oxford University Press, 2016.

Heredia, Luisa. "From Prayer to Protest: The Immigrant Rights Movement and the Catholic Church." In *Rallying for Immigrant Rights: The Fight for Inclusion in 21st Century America,* edited by Kim Voss and Irene Bloemraad, 101–122. Berkeley: University of California Press, 2011.

Hill Collins, Patricia. "Intersectionality's Definitional Dilemmas." *Annual Review of Sociology* 41 (2015): 1–20.

Hill Collins, Patricia, and Sirma Bilge. *Intersectionality.* Hoboken, NJ: Wiley, 2016.

Holston, James, ed. *Cities and Citizenship.* Durham, NC: Duke University Press, 1998.

Hondagneu-Sotelo, Pierette. *Domestica: Immigrant Women Workers Cleaning and Caring in the Shadows of Affluence.* Berkeley: University of California Press, 2001.

———. *Gender and U.S. Immigration: Contemporary Trends.* Berkeley: University of California Press, 2003.

———. *Gendered Transitions: Mexican Experiences of Immigration.* Berkeley: University of California Press, 1994.

———. "New Directions in Gender and Immigration Research." In *The Routledge International Handbook of Migration Studies,* edited by Stephen Gold and Stephanie Nawyn, 180–188. New York: Routledge, 2012.

———, ed. *Religion and Social Justice for Immigrants.* New Brunswick, NJ: Rutgers University Press, 2007.

Hondagneu-Sotelo, Pierette, and Ernestine Avila. "'I'm Here, but I'm There': The Meanings of Latina Transnational Motherhood." *Gender and Society* 11, no. 5 (1997): 548–571.

Hull, Kathleen. *Same-Sex Marriage: The Cultural Politics of Love and Law.* New York: Cambridge University Press, 2006.

Jasper, James. "A Strategic Approach to Collective Action: Looking for Agency in Social-Movement Choices." *Mobilization* 9, no. 1 (2004): 1–16.

Keating, Cricket. "Building Coalitional Consciousness." *NWSA Journal* 17, no. 2 (2005): 86–103.

Kolenz, Kristen A., Krista L. Benson, Judy Tzu-Chun Wu, Leslie Bow, Avtar Brah, Mishuana Goeman, Diane Harriford, Shari M. Huhndorf, Analouise Keating, Yi-Chun Tricia Lin, Laura Pérez, Zenaida Peterson, Becky Thompson, and Tiffany Willoughby-Herard. "Combahee River Collective Statement: A Fortieth Anniversary Retrospective." *Frontiers: A Journal of Women's Studies* 38, no. 3 (2017): 164–189.

Kurtz, Sharon. *Workplace Justice: Organizing Multi-identity Movements.* Minneapolis: University of Minnesota Press, 2002.

Lamont, Michèle, and Virág Molnár. "The Study of Boundaries in the Social Sciences." *Annual Review of Sociology* 28 (2002): 167–195.

Leachman, Gwendolyn M. "From Protest to *Perry*: How Litigation Shaped the LGBT Movement's Agenda." *UC Davis Law Review* 47 (2014): 1667–1751.

Lee, Erika. *At America's Gates: Chinese Immigration during the Exclusion Era, 1882–1943*. Chapel Hill: University of North Carolina Press, 2003.

Leon, Lucia Praxedia. "Marriage and Legalization: Legal Consciousness of Latina/o Young Adults Navigating Marriage-Based Legalization Pathways." Ms. 2017. https://escholarship.org.

López, Jane Lily. "'Impossible Families': Mixed-Citizenship Status Couples and the Law." *Law and Policy* 37 (2015): 93–118.

Lubhéid, Ethine. *Entry Denied: Controlling Sexuality at the Border*. Minneapolis: University of Minnesota Press, 2002.

Lubhéid, Ethine, and Lionel Cantú Jr., eds. *Queer Migrations: Sexuality, U.S. Citizenship and Border Crossings*. Minneapolis: University of Minnesota Press, 2005.

Luna, Zakiya. "'Truly a Women of Color Organization': Negotiating Sameness and Difference in Pursuit of Intersectionality." *Gender and Society* 30, no. 5 (2016): 769–790.

Maira, Sunaina. *Missing: Youth, Citizenship and Empire after 9/11*. Durham, NC: Duke University Press, 2009.

Maney, George, M., Kenneth T. Andrews, Rachel V. Kutz-Flamenbaum, Deana A. Rohlinger, and Jeff Goodwin. "An Introduction to Strategies for Social Change." In *Strategies for Social Change*, edited by Gregory M. Maney, Rachel V. Kutz-Flamenbaum, Deana A. Rohlinger, and Jeff Goodwin, 17. Minneapolis: University of Minnesota Press, 2012.

Mansbridge, Jane, and Aldon Morris, eds. *Oppositional Consciousness: The Subjective Roots of Social Protest*. Chicago: University of Chicago Press, 2001.

Marcus, George E. "Ethnography in/of the World System: The Emergence of Multi-sited Ethnography." *Annual Review of Anthropology* 24 (1995): 95–117.

Marshall, Anna-Maria. *Confronting Sexual Harassment: The Law and Politics of Everyday Life*. Burlington, VT: Dartmouth Ashgate, 2005.

McAdam, Doug. "Recruitment to High-Risk Activism: The Case of Freedom Summer." *American Journal of Sociology* 92, no. 1 (1986): 64–90.

McCammon, Holly. *The U.S. Women's Jury Movements and Strategic Adaptation: A More Just Verdict*. New York: Cambridge University Press, 2012.

McCann, Michael. "Law and Social Movements: Contemporary Perspectives." *Annual Review of Law and Social Science* 2 (2006): 17–38.

———. *Rights at Work: Pay Equity Reform and the Politics of Legal Mobilization*. Chicago: University of Chicago Press, 1994.

Mendez, Jennifer Bickham. "Globalizing Scholar Activism: Opportunities and Dilemmas through a Feminist Lens." In *Engaging Contradictions: Theory, Politics and Methods of Activist Scholarship*, edited by Charles R. Hale, 136–163. Berkeley: University of California Press, 2008.

Menjívar, Cecilia, and Leisy Abrego. "Legal Violence: Immigration Law and the Lives of Central American Immigrants." *American Journal of Sociology* 117, no. 5 (2012): 1380–1421.

Menjívar, Cecilia, and Daniel Kanstroom, eds. *Constructing Immigrant "Illegality": Critiques, Experiences and Responses*. New York: Cambridge University Press, 2014.

Menjívar, Cecilia, and Sarah M. Lakhani. "Transformative Effects of Immigration Law: Migrants' Personal and Social Metamorphoses through Regularization." *American Journal of Sociology* 121, no. 6 (2016): 1818–1855.

Merry, Sally Engle, Peggy Levitt, Mihaela Serban Rosen, and Diana Yoon. "Law from Below: Women's Human Rights and Social Movements in New York City." *Law and Society Review* 44, no. 1 (2010): 101–128.

Molina, Natalia. *How Race Is Made in America: Immigration, Citizenship, and the Historical Power of Racial Scripts*. Berkeley: University of California Press, 2014.

Montejano, David. *Quixote's Soldiers: A Local History of the Chicano Movement, 1966–1981* Austin: University of Texas Press, 2010.

Moon, Dawne. "Who Am I and Who Are We? Conflicting Narratives of Collective Selfhood in Stigmatized Groups." *American Journal of Sociology* 117, no. 5 (2012): 1336–1379.

Moss, Dana. "Transnational Repression, Diaspora Mobilization, and the Case of the Arab Spring." Social Problems 63, no. 4 (2016): 480–498.

Munkres, Susan. "Being Sisters to Salvadoran Peasants." In *Identity Work in Social Movements*, edited by Jo Reger, Daniel J. Myers, and Rachel L. Einwohner, 189–212. Minneapolis: University of Minnesota Press, 2008.

Muñoz, Susana María, and Marta María Maldonado. "Counterstories of College Persistence by Undocumented Mexicana Students: Navigating Race, Class, Gender and Legal Status." *International Journal of Qualitative Studies in Education* 25, no. 3 (2012): 293–315.

Myers, Daniel. "Ally Identity." In *Identity Work in Social Movements*, edited by Jo Reger, Daniel J. Myers, and Rachel L. Einwohner, 167–188. Minneapolis: University of Minnesota Press, 2008.

Nader, Laura. "Up the Anthropologist: Perspectives Gained from Studying Up." In *Reinventing Anthropology*, edited by Dell Hymes, 284–311. 1969; New York: Vintage Books, 1974.

Nakano Glenn, Evelyn. *Forced to Care: Coercion and Caregiving in America*. Cambridge, MA: Harvard University Press, 2012.

Nash, Jennifer. *Black Feminism Reimagined: After Intersectionality*. Durham, NC: Duke University Press, 2019.

NeJaime, Douglas. "Winning through Losing." *Iowa Law Review* 96, no. 3 (2011): 941–1012.

Ngai, Mae. *Impossible Subjects: Illegal Aliens and the Making of Modern America*. Princeton, NJ: Princeton University Press, 2004.

Nicholls, Walter. *The DREAMers: How the Undocumented Youth Movement Transformed the Immigrant Rights Debate*. Stanford, CA: Stanford University Press, 2013.

Nicholls, Walter, and Justus Uitermark. *Cities and Social Movements: Immigrant Rights Activism in the United States, France, and the Netherlands, 1970–2015*. Hoboken, NJ: Wiley-Blackwell, 2017.

Nishida, Akemi. "Understanding Political Development through an Intersectionality Framework." *Disability Studies Quarterly* 36, no. 2 (2016).

Olivas, Michael. *No Undocumented Child Left Behind: Plyler v. Doe and the Education of Undocumented Schoolchildren.* New York: New York University Press, 2012.

Pallares, Amalia. *Family Activism: Immigrant Struggles and the Politics of Noncitizenship.* New Brunswick, NJ: Rutgers University Press, 2015.

Pallares, Amalia, and Nilda Flores-González, eds. *Marcha! Latino Chicago and the Immigrant Rights Movement.* Urbana: University of Illinois Press, 2010.

Parreñas, Rhacel Salazar. "Transnational Mothering: A Source of Gender Conflicts in the Family." *University of North Carolina Law Review* 88 (2010): 1825–1855.

Passel, Jeffrey S., and D'Vera Cohn. "Unauthorized Immigrant Population: National and State Trends, 2010." Washington, DC: Pew Hispanic Research Center, February 2011. www.pewhispanic.org.

Patler, Caitlin. "Racialized Illegality: The Convergence of Race and Legal Status among Black, Latino and Asian-American Undocumented Young Adults." In *Scholars and Southern California Immigrants in Dialogue: New Conversations in Public Sociology,* edited by Victoria Carty, Rafael Luévano, and Tekle Woldemikael, 93–114. Lanham, MD: Lexington Press, 2014.

Pérez Huber, Lindsay. "Healing Images and Narratives: Undocumented Chicana/ Latina Pedagogies of Resistance." *Journal of Latinos and Education* 16, no. 4 (2017): 374–389.

———. "Using Latina/o Critical Race Theory (LatCrit) and Racist Nativism to Explore Intersectionality in the Educational Experiences of Undocumented Chicana College Students." *Journal of Educational Foundations* 24, no. 1 (2010): 77–96.

Perez Huber, Lindsay, Corina Benavides Lopez, Maria C. Malagon, Veronica Velez, and Daniel G. Solórzano. "Getting beyond the 'Symptom,' Acknowledging the 'Disease': Theorizing Racist Nativism." *Contemporary Justice Review* 11 (2008): 39–51.

Pila, Daniela. "'I'm Not Good Enough for Anyone': Legal Status and the Dating Lives of Undocumented Young Adults." *Sociological Forum* 31, no. 1 (2016): 138–158.

Polletta, Francesca. *It Was Like a Fever: Storytelling in Protest and Politics.* Chicago: University of Chicago Press, 2006.

Polletta, Francesca, Pang Ching Bobby Chen, Beth Charity Gardner, and Alice Motes. "The Sociology of Storytelling." *Annual Review of Sociology* 37 (2011): 109–130.

Polletta, Francesca, and James Jasper. "Collective Identity and Social Movements." *Annual Review of Sociology* 27 (2001): 283–305.

Provine, Doris Marie, Monica W. Varsanyi, Paul G. Lewis, and Scott H. Decker. *Policing Immigrants: Local Law Enforcement on the Front Lines.* Chicago: University of Chicago Press, 2016.

Puar, Jasbir. *Terrorist Assemblages: Homonationalism in Queer Times.* Durham, NC: Duke University Press, 2007.

Pulido, Laura. *Black, Brown, Yellow, and Left: Radical Activism in Los Angeles.* Berkeley: University of California Press, 2006.

Reger, Jo, Daniel J. Myers, and Rachel L. Einwohner, eds. *Identity Work in Social Movements.* Minneapolis: University of Minnesota Press, 2008.

Roberts, Dorothy, and Sujatha Jesudason. "Movement Intersectionality: The Case of Race, Gender, Disability and Genetic Technologies." *DuBois Review* 10, no. 2 (2013): 313–328.

Romero, Mary. "Constructing Mexican Immigrant Women as a Threat to American Families." *International Journal of Sociology of the Family* 37, no. 1 (2011): 49–68.

Romero, Robert Chao. "Transnational Chinese Immigrant Smuggling to the United States via Mexico and Cuba, 1882–1916." *Amerasia* 30, no. 3 (2004): 1–16.

Roque Ramirez, Horacio N. "Claiming Queer Cultural Citizenship: Gay Latino (Im) Migrant Acts in San Francisco." In *Queer Migrations: Sexuality, U.S. Citizenship and Border Crossings*, edited by Ethine Lubhéid and Lionel Cantú Jr., 161–188. Minneapolis: University of Minnesota Press, 2005.

Rosenberg, Gerald. *The Hollow Hope: Can Courts Bring About Social Change?* Chicago: University of Chicago Press, 2008.

Ross, Loretta J. "Reproductive Justice as Intersectional Feminist Activism." *Souls: A Critical Journal of Black Politics, Culture and Society* 18 (2017): 286–314.

Rumbaut, Rubén. "Generation 1.5, Educational Experiences of." In *Encyclopedia of Diversity in Education*, edited by James A. Banks. Thousand Oaks: Sage, 2012.

Russo, Chandra. "Allies Forging a Collective Identity: Embodiment and Emotions on the Migrant Trail." *Mobilization* 19, no. 1 (2014): 67–82.

Ruszczyk, Stephen, and Guillermo Yrizar Barbosa. "A Second Generation of Immigrant Illegality Studies." *Migration Studies* 5, no. 3 (2016): 445–456.

Salcido, Olivia, and Cecilia Menjívar. "Gendered Paths to Legal Citizenship: The Case of Latin-American Immigrants in Phoenix, Arizona." *Law and Society Review* 46, no. 2 (2012): 335–368.

Sarachild, Kathie. "Consciousness-Raising: A Radical Weapon." In *Notes from Feminist Revolution: Redstockings of the Women's Liberation Movement*, edited by Kathie Sarachild, 144–150. New York: Random House, 1978.

Sassen, Saskia. "The Global City: Introducing a Concept." *Brown Journal of World Affairs* 11, no. 2 (2005): 27–43.

Seif, Hinda. "'Coming Out of the Shadows' and 'Undocuqueer.'" *Journal of Language and Sexuality* 3, no. 1 (2014): 87–120.

Shah, Bijal. "LGBT Identity in Immigration." *Columbia Human Rights Law Review* 45 (2013): 100–213.

Stryker, Sheldon, Timothy J. Owens, and Robert W. White, eds. *Self, Identity, and Social Movements*. Minneapolis: University of Minnesota Press, 2000.

Swerts, Thomas. "Gaining a Voice: Storytelling and Undocumented Youth Activism in Chicago." *Mobilization* 20, no. 3 (2015): 345–360.

Swidler, Anne. "Culture in Action: Symbols and Strategies." *American Sociological Review* 51, no. 2 (1986): 273–286.

Taylor, Verta, and Nancy Whittier. "Collective Identity in Social Movement Communities: Lesbian Feminist Mobilization." In *Frontiers in Social Movement Theory*, edited by Aldon D. Morris and Carol McClug Mueller, 104–130. New Haven, CT: Yale University Press, 1992.

Terriquez, Veronica. "Intersectional Mobilization, Social Movement Spillover, and Queer Youth Leadership in the Immigrant Rights Movement." *Social Problems* 62, no. 3 (2015): 343–362.

Terriquez, Veronica, Tizoc Brenes, and Abidel Lopez. "Intersectionality as a Multipurpose Collective Action Frame: The Case of the Undocumented Youth Movement." *Ethnicities* 18, no. 2 (2018): 260–276.

Tilly, Charles. *Regimes and Repertoires*. Chicago: University of Chicago Press, 2010.

Tilly, Charles, and Sidney Tarrow. *Contentious Politics*. Boulder, CO: Paradigm, 2007.

Tomchin, Olga. "Bodies and Bureaucracy: Legal Sex Classification and Marriage-Based Immigration for Trans* People." *California Law Review* 101, no. 3 (2013): 813–862.

Tomlinson, Barbara, and George Lipsitz. "American Studies as Accompaniment." *American Quarterly* 65, no. 1 (2013): 1–30.

Valdez, Zulema, and Tanya Golash-Boza. "Master Status or Intersectional Identity? Undocumented Students' Sense of Belonging on a College Campus." *Identities* (2018): 1–19.

Van Dyke, Nella, and Holly J. McCammon, eds. *Strategic Alliances: Coalition Building and Social Movements*. Minneapolis: University of Minnesota Press, 2010.

Villazor, Rose Cuison. "'Sanctuary Cities' and Local Citizenship." *Fordham Urban Law Journal* 37 (2010): 573–598.

———. "The Undocumented Closet." *University of North Carolina Law Review* 92 (2013): 1–74.

Voss, Kim, and Irene Bloemraad, eds. *Rallying for Immigrant Rights: The Fight for Inclusion in 21ˢᵗ Century America*. Berkeley: University of California Press, 2011.

Waters, Mary C. *Black Identities: West Indian Immigrant Dreams and American Realities*. Cambridge, MA: Harvard University Press, 2001.

Whittier, Nancy. "Identity Politics, Consciousness-Raising and Visibility Politics." In *The Oxford Handbook of U.S. Women's Social Movement Activism*, edited by Holly McCammon, Verta Taylor, Jo Reger, and Rachel Einwohner, 376–397. New York: Oxford University Press, 2017.

———. "The Politics of Visibility: Coming Out and Individual and Collective Identity," in *Strategies for Social Change*, edited by Jeff Goodwin, Rachel Kutz-Flamenbaum, Greg Maney, and Deana Rohlinger, 184–208. Minneapolis: University of Minnesota Press, 2012.

Willen, Sarah. "Toward a Critical Phenomenology of Illegality: State Power, Criminalization, and Abjectivity among Undocumented Migrant Workers in Tel Aviv, Israel." *International Migration* 45, no. 3 (2007): 8–38.

Wong, Kent, Janna Shadduck-Hernandez, Fabiola Inzunza, Julie Monroe, Victor Narro, and Abel Valenzuela Jr., eds. *Undocumented and Unafraid: Tam Tran, Cynthia Felix and the Immigrant Youth Movement*. Los Angeles: UCLA Labor Center, 2012.

Wu, Ellen. *The Model Minority Myth: Asian Americans and the Origins of the Model Minority*. Princeton, NJ: Princeton University Press, 2015.

Yoshikawa, Hirokazu. *Immigrants Raising Citizens: Undocumented Parents and Their Young Children*. New York: Russell Sage Foundation, 2011.

Yoshino, Kenji. "Assimilation Bias in Equal Protection: The Visibility Presumption and the Case of Don't Ask, Don't Tell." *Yale Law Journal* 108 (1998): 485–571.

Yuval-Davis, Nira. "Intersectionality and Feminist Politics." *European Journal of Women's Studies* 13, no. 3 (2009): 193–209.

Zavella, Patricia. "Intersectional Praxis in the Movement for Reproductive Justice: The Respect ABQ Women Campaign." *Signs* 42, no. 2 (2017): 509–533.

Zepeda-Millán, Chris. *Latino Mass Mobilization: Immigration, Racialization, and Activism.* New York: Cambridge University Press, 2017.

Zimmerman, Arely. "Transmedia Testimonio: Examining Undocumented Youth's Political Activism in the Digital Age." *International Journal of Communication* 10 (2016): 1886–1906.

INDEX

Tables are indicated by a t following the page reference.

ABOUT THE AUTHOR

Kevin Escudero is Assistant Professor of American Studies and Ethnic Studies at Brown University.